AFRICA'S RED HARVEST

PIETER LESSING

Africa's Red Harvest

THE JOHN DAY COMPANY

NEW YORK

CONTENTS

FOREWORD

References to Soviet bloc activities in Africa appear almost daily in the newspapers. In spite of that it is difficult, even for anybody interested in the subject, to follow the course of events. The mere size of Africa makes understanding difficult. Something happening in Senegal cannot easily be related to an incident in Tanganyika, 4,000 miles away.

The political developments in Rhodesia are completely different from the inter-African struggle in Ghana, which has been independent for five years. In Angola the Africans are attacking the Portuguese; in the Cameroun Republic they are fighting their own independent African Government.

In Tanganyika Julius Nyerere resigns, and in Gabon, on the other side of the continent, the Africans demand that their Prime Minister should follow Nyerere's example, although there is no apparent contact between the two countries. Is there any connection?

Arms manufactured in Czechoslovakia are found in Angola. Almost simultaneously it is found that a number of Africans from the Cameroun Republic have received military training in Communist China. Again: is there any connection? Are Russia and China working together in Africa as a team?

In Nigeria the trade unions have split; in Kenya the Federation of Labour is getting restive and threatening to split in an identical way. But conditions in Nigeria are entirely different from those prevailing in Kenya. Is there, somehow, a link between the trade unions of the two countries?

Is there, in short, a discernible pattern which underlies some of the otherwise inexplicable happenings in Africa?

In trying to find an answer an immediate problem is that

7

although the actual events in Africa receive wide publicity, little is known of what goes on behind the scenes. I believe that I am not the only person who has found many of the developments in Africa perplexing if taken at their face value, or who has found that some of the people who talk most and loudest about the current African scene are those with the least overall concept of the interplay that is going on.

Few efforts have been made to present an outline of the course the struggle for Africa is following, of the form the Communist infiltration is taking and of its failure or success.

This book is an unambitious attempt to give one aspect of the picture, the aspect in which the Communist drive is face to face with black Africa's own aspirations. It does not deal with the Arab countries of the north; reference to them is made only when developments there are relevant to the struggle in the new countries of Africa.

The problem of finding the facts has been great. There was no official or unofficial overall brief to which I had access; as far as I could discover no brief exists which fits together all Communist bloc activities over the whole of Africa, and which draws conclusions from them.

I have been fortunate in being given access to sources which, to my regret, I cannot disclose, and of receiving the co-operation of persons and organisations who must, similarly, remain un-identified for reasons which are self-evident. One source which I can disclose and to which I am greatly indebted is the Central Research Unit of the B.B.C., and I would like to pay special tribute to the work of Mr Walter Kolarz. The views expressed and the interpretation of certain facts are, of course, my own.

A danger when writing about the Communist infiltration in Africa is the temptation to see a Russian or a Communist agent behind every African tree. Those who accuse me of that will find my answer in Chapter Thirteen as well as in parts of other chapters. I hope I have also made it quite clear that I do not confuse genuine African nationalism with Communism.

This is not a guide book to Communism in Africa. It is no more than an attempt to help people who have a genuine interest in the struggle which is now being waged in black Africa, and which is about to become very intense, to read the signs with some clarity. My hope is that it will be of help to those who seek to understand the warnings which come almost daily from Africa.

Chapter One was originally intended as an introduction, but it became too long. It nevertheless stands apart from the rest of the book and is the only instance in which I deal in detail with the events in a particular country, although not with the politics of that country. I have throughout tried to avoid discussing internal African politics, but have been unable to do so altogether.

1

SUBSTITUTE
FOR AN INTRODUCTION

On March 10th 1961 a movement called the *Uniao das Populaçoes de Angola* (U.P.A.) issued, from its headquarters at 78 rue Dodoma, Leopoldville, a call for a general strike in Northern Angola, to take place five days later on March 15th. On the night of the 15th the Security Council in New York was due to vote on a resolution condemning Portugal for her African policy. The strike was to coincide with that.

In a few areas near the Congo frontier the strike did take place, but did not get the expected publicity, largely because of the inadequacy of news communications in Angola. Twenty-four hours later it had been overshadowed by a far more serious event: at about the time the vote was taken in the Security Council, a terrorist army had swept across the frontier from the Congo into Angola in a 50-prong attack along a 400-mile front, killing Africans and Portuguese, men, women and children, indiscriminately.

During the previous few days this army had moved from Thysville in the Congo, about sixty miles north of the frontier (and about an equal distance south of Leopoldville), where it had been undergoing training of sorts for about six months. It was at the time of the invasion not well equipped, but owing to the element of surprise it was able within a matter of days to overrun an impressively large area, and it was to continue sustained operations which were still in progress by the end of the year.

Since the night of March 15th 1961, the rights and wrongs of this army's activities have been debated in every corner of the world, as have been the accounts of atrocities and counter atrocities.

I should state quite clearly that I am not taking part in that controversy. I am prepared to accept that there was brutality on both sides. Neither is this an attempt to discuss Portuguese rule in Angola. I propose to deal with only one aspect of the bloodshed: was this a spontaneous uprising or was it engineered by interests outside Angola?

The rebel story, as told by their military commander, Holden Roberto, who is the leader of the U.P.A. and the self-styled Commander-in-Chief of the 'Army of Liberation,' is that the strike ordered for March 15th was totally effective. According to him the Portuguese authorities tried to break it with what he calls their customary brutality. After a number of strikers had been shot, the brow-beaten Africans at last turned and hit back in self-defence. The help that came from outside was a desperate rescue operation, the story continues. Roberto also denies most emphatically that any link exists between his movement and any Communist body.

But on December 7th 1960, three months before the uprising, the *People's Daily*, the official Chinese organ published in Peking, commenting on the Communist Summit which had ended in Moscow on December 1st, stated that the next phase in the 'liberation' of Africa had been considered at the Moscow meeting. It added that the next task to be undertaken was the liberation of Angola, to be followed by a fight for independence in Portuguese Guinea, and that the call had gone out to 'rise and fight.'

Two days after the end of the Moscow summit a call had in fact been issued by the U.P.A. from Leopoldville. Dated December 3rd 1960, it read in part:

'Long live U.P.A. Long live Nikita Khrushchev. Long live

Angola . . . Prepare your arms. We are about to open fire. We have no fear. Russia will provide weapons and Lumumba will help us. Let us kill the whites. Lumumba has given the authority.'

Inflammatory Communist radio propaganda beamed to the Portuguese territories of Africa began six months before the uprising. That it was the beginning of a systematic campaign to prepare for the coming upheaval has since become clear, but at that time it seemed puzzling that precious radio time was being devoted to relatively quiet Mozambique and Angola at the expense of propaganda to the Congo, for instance, or to Cameroun, East Africa or Somalia.

In any event the broadcasts in Portuguese started in September 1960. China was first in the field and by the middle of 1961 was devoting seven hours a week to broadcasts beamed to Angola. In Europe, Russia at first left it to Czechoslovakia and Rumania to carry on the radio campaign, with Radio Prague and Radio Bucharest each devoting three and a half hours a week to it.

Only in August 1961 did Moscow Radio itself begin transmissions in Portuguese beamed to Angola, giving them for a short period of seven hours a week. The service has since been cut to three and a half hours a week, the rest of the time being added to an Amharic service beamed to Ethiopia.

THE PREPARATIONS

The story of the uprising in Angola appears to have started nearly one year earlier, with the arrival of Daniel Semenovich Solod in Conakry, the capital of Guinea, as Soviet Ambassador. Solod is one of the Soviet Union's most able diplomats. In the immediate post-war years he served in Syria and Lebanon as head of the Soviet Mission. In 1950 he became Deputy Head of the Near and Middle East Department of the Soviet Ministry for Foreign Affairs, a position he retained after his appointment in 1954 as Ambassador to Egypt.

Under Solod the Soviet Embassy in Cairo became the centre for Russian agitation in the Middle East and North Africa. Solod was in fact in control of Russian relations with Ethiopia, the Sudan, Turkey, Syria, Lebanon, Jordan, Egypt, Libya, Tunisia and Morocco. His success in spreading Soviet influence throughout the Middle East and North Africa has never been disputed.

In 1956 he returned to Moscow to become Acting Head of the Near and Middle East Department of the Soviet Foreign Ministry.

A brilliant organiser, Solod is recognised as an expert in infiltration and subversion. Significantly, on his appointment to Conakry he did not relinquish his previous position in the Soviet Foreign Ministry. (That he subsequently quarrelled with President Sekou Touré of Guinea and was expelled has no relevance in this context.)

Until Solod's arrival in Conakry there was no evidence of a concerted Soviet drive in West Africa. Although close relations had been established with Guinea, although contact between Ghana and Russia was increasing and although there were isolated attempts to establish bridgeheads, such as in the Cameroun Republic, it was not a co-ordinated operation. The year 1960 was to change that, and Solod's arrival in Conakry marked the beginning of the change. He immediately took control of Soviet operations along Africa's Atlantic coast.

Among the countries earmarked for attention was Angola. Russian thinking was possibly influenced by an assumption that strong Soviet representation in the Congo, whose independence was approaching, would give easy access to Angola.

Soon after his arrival in Conakry, Solod established contact with a number of Angola Africans living outside Angola. The three most important are:

MARIO PINTO DE ANDRADE

Born in Cuanza Norte, Angola, in 1928, de Andrade was already well known in Communist circles. He was educated mainly in Portugal where he graduated at the *Faculdade de Letras* in Lisbon before studying sociology in Paris and Frankfurt. While a student in Lisbon he joined the underground Portuguese Communist Party and later became a member also of the French Communist Party. In 1955 he left France to continue his studies first in Warsaw and then in Moscow. After that trace was lost of him until 1958 when he was a delegate to the Afro-Asian Writers' Conference which Russia had convened at Tashkent, in Uzbekistan, Soviet Asia.

That same year he was in slight trouble with the French police who found on him documents which established that he had been in close touch with Peking for some time. He has since been a contributor to *Pravda* and other Communist publications.

There is no evidence that de Andrade at any time returned to Angola. From 1959 he had been resident in Conakry where he became the head of a movement called the *Movimento Popular para a Libertaçao de Angola* (M.P.L.A.). It appears that he was on terms of friendship with President Sekou Touré by the time Solod arrived.

HOLDEN ROBERTO

Also known as José Gilmore, Ruy Ventura, Robert Haldane and Onofre, Holden Roberto is his real name. Born in San Salvador, Northern Angola, in 1923, the son of a Christian African peasant, he was named after an American Protestant missionary, a Dr Holden. Educated at a mission school in what was then the Belgian Congo, his association with Belgian Communists is believed to have started soon after he left school. In subsequent years in France he became closely identified with the French Communist Party. Roberto also spent a short time in Britain and in fact married an English girl, Susan Milton.

In 1954 he returned to Leopoldville and shortly afterwards formed the U.P.A., at that time a small movement, which gained the support of members of the short-lived Angola Communist Party after the latter had disbanded for tactical reasons. Roberto's main function in Leopoldville was to organise the distribution of Communist propaganda in the Portuguese territories. He subsequently won the interest and sympathy of President Nkrumah and President Sekou Touré.

VIRIATO FRANCISCO CLEMENTE DA CRUZ

Born in Angola in 1928, da Cruz studied in Paris where he joined the French Communist Party. In 1952, when he became the organiser of a group known as the 'New Intellectuals of Angola,' he described himself as being 'absolutely possessed by a Communist mentality.' He has often visited London where he has many connections. Conakry has been his home since 1959.

By the middle of 1960 Roberto's U.P.A. was put on a new footing. With the help of advisers from Conakry the cell system was introduced, with members knowing the identity of only two or three other members. Cell leaders received their training in the Congo, and a substantial membership was recruited from Angola Africans living there. Many of them had been away from Angola for many years, some since childhood, but now they returned as recruiting agents for their respective cells.

Meanwhile the movement which de Andrade had founded in Conakry, the M.P.L.A., also began to flourish. This was, however, a political rather than a military organisation and its function was to establish liaison with Communist movements and front organisations in other parts of the world.

While Roberto was engaged during 1960 in building up his

'Army of Liberation,' de Andrade and da Cruz spent much of their time in Russia and other Iron Curtain countries. There is evidence that arrangements were made by them for arms to be supplied to Roberto from the Lenin works at Pilsen (the former Skoda works). There was, however, a hitch in the delivery of these arms at a crucial moment which caused much friction between de Andrade and Roberto. Jealousy was also to develop between the two.

'The Devil Will Help'

The American Committee for Africa and the British Movement for the Freedom of the Peoples in the Portuguese Colonies have both tried to present the friction between Roberto and de Andrade as a result of ideological differences. Roberto is projected in the West as anti-Communist but this is disproved by an Order-of-the-Day he issued on the eve of the terrorist outbreak. I have a photostat copy of it.

Marked 'Strictly Secret' and addressed to 'Dear Compatriots of Angola,' it is, significantly, in French. The Angola Africans who are said to have risen spontaneously cannot speak or understand French; an army moving from Thysville in the Congo, on the other hand, would be able to understand it.

After the usual exhortations to fight well and after hailing the martyred Lumumba, the Order goes on:

'Kwame Nkrumah and Sekou Touré are at our side. Five million have been delivered to get the necessary means to conquer and liberate Angola.'

Then, after warning against 'tribalists' who are not in the fight, Roberto goes on: 'Here, in a few words, is our plan for the future. Sekou Touré will reign over the northern part of (West) Africa, Comrade Nkrumah will rule the centre and your servant Holden Roberto the south. We hope that our eminent comrade "THE DEVIL" will help us to realise our destiny.

'The future is being forged. You must not believe those who spread nonsense. Communism is not bad. When we stayed in Moscow we were able to see for ourselves many wonderful things which the West will never have.'

The Order concludes: 'Our comrade THE DEVIL is standing by with a watchful eye. LONG LIVE COMMUNISM. DOWN WITH CONCENTRIC TRIBALISM.'

The reference to 'five million' is assumed to refer to money. 'The Devil' is a code name and possibly refers to Russia.

Nevertheless friction did develop between him and de Andrade. This became evident when, in 1960, the *Front Révolutionnaire Africain Pour l'Indépendance Nationale des Colonies Portugaises* (F.R.A.I.N.) was created at the instigation of Solod, with headquarters in Conakry.

Ostensibly representing all movements in Portuguese Africa striving for independence, the two key persons in it were de Andrade and a self-confessed Communist from Portuguese Guinea, Amilcar Lopes Cabral, who had shortly before returned from Moscow. On de Andrade's insistence Roberto was given no representation on this co-ordinating body, de Andrade's assumption being that Roberto was his junior and had to take orders from him.

This was de Andrade's attitude as late as May 1961 when, addressing a rally on a visit to Peking, he claimed that Roberto (to whom he referred as Gilmore) acted only on his instructions and had no independent command.

Buying Arms

De Andrade's position had, however, been weakened since the beginning of the uprising. This was because of bitter complaints from Roberto that the arms which had been promised, and whose distribution was the immediate responsibility of de Andrade, were not reaching him in sufficient quantities although adequate deliveries had arrived in Guinea and Ghana.

Roberto's complaints were justified. The terrorist army that invaded Angola on March 15th was badly equipped – with old, often home-made, rifles and machetes. What modern rifles it had Roberto had himself obtained from the Congolese Army and in some cases from United Nations troops. It is not suggested that the U.N. in New York knew about this but there were many instances of United Nations troops selling their rifles and ammunition.

Members of the Congolese Army were and still are notorious for the ease with which they can be persuaded to sell their weapons. Roberto was a ready buyer. But his complaints to Solod in Conakry did not fall on deaf ears and for a short, crucial period advisers from Solod's Embassy personally supervised deliveries and distribution. Soviet trawlers in fact carried arms from Conakry direct to the Angola coast. This was, however, a practice too dangerous to continue for long and was undertaken only as an emergency operation until better supply lines could be organised through Ghana.

By early May large-scale gun-running through Ghana was working satisfactorily, with Soviet and Polish ships bringing supplies direct to the Ghanaian port of Takoradi. From May, therefore, Roberto's forces were equipped with modern Czech automatic weapons and two-way radio communications.

Attempts to Create a United Front

Solod appears also to have become dissatisfied with the relatively unimportant status de Andrade had given Roberto. He therefore urged the setting up of a new, truly representative resistance front. The first steps to create this were taken at a meeting which took place in Casablanca from April 18th to 20th, 1961. Called the 'Conference of Nationalist Movements of the Portuguese Colonies,' it was attended by both a Russian and a Chinese delegation and by observers from Ghana, Guinea, Morocco and Egypt.

The outcome was a permanent secretariat for all resistance movements, based on Conakry, and a consultative council on which all resistance leaders have a vote. De Andrade was appointed secretary-general, but he did not retain the power to act as overlord. He became merely a co-ordinator.

Another result of the conference was the creation of the *Frente Comum dos Partidos Angolanos em Leopoldville* (Common Front of Angola Parties in Leopoldville). Predominant among the member organisations of this front is Roberto's U.P.A. De Andrade has, however, brought his original movement, the M.P.L.A., into this common front which now also includes three other small movements, the *Association des Ressortissants de l'Enclave de Cabinda* (A.R.E.C.), which seeks independence for the small Portuguese enclave at the mouth of the Congo or its affiliation with the Congo, the *Ngwiza Kongo* (N.G.W.I.Z.A.C.O.), which wants the reunification of all the territories at the mouth of the Congo, and the *Aliança dos Naturais de Maquela do Zombo* (A.L.I.A.Z.O.), which demands the return of the Angola province of Bazombo to its 'ethnic origin,' presumably the Congo.

The effect of the reorganisation has been that Roberto is recognised as fully in charge of military operations in Angola and not subservient to de Andrade. Moreover, it has been accepted that Roberto's fight (and his needs) should take precedence over those of resistance movements in other parts of Portuguese Africa.

Confirmation of this came in an intercepted letter from the Soviet Committee of Afro-Asian Solidarity addressed to the 'Permanent Secretariat of the Nationalist Organisations of the Portuguese Colonies.'

Signed by Lev Souhanov on behalf of the Soviet Committee, the letter reads in part (it is in French): 'Dear friends, We herewith inform you that we have received the resolution and the discussions . . . of the Casablanca meeting of 18th to 20th April 1961. We are using all these documents as well as others which are at our disposal . . . We are accordingly sending you herewith the resolution concerning Angola adopted by the Presidium of our committee on May 8th. This resolution has been published in various Soviet newspapers and transmitted by radio to Africa . . . We also wish to inform you that our committee has started a large organisation in the U.S.S.R. to support the fighting Angola people and all peoples under Portuguese domination . . .'

The resolution which was enclosed greeted 'the courageous patriots of Angola' on behalf of 220 million people in the Soviet Union, demanded the immediate independence of Angola and appealed 'to all people of goodwill in the entire world to offer all help within their means to the fighting people of Angola.'

Further confirmation came from Mr Khrushchev himself. The delegates meeting in Casablanca had sent Khrushchev a message asking for his support for the peoples in the Portuguese territories in Africa. His reply (dated June 19th – nearly two months later) reads in part: 'The Soviet Government and the Soviet people . . . are ready to render utmost aid and support in this just struggle of the people of Angola . . . The patriots of Angola can rest assured that . . . the Soviet Union is promoting an extensive drive to expose the criminal actions of the Portuguese colonialists in Angola and to increase support for the struggling people of Angola.'

Khrushchev made no reference to the other Portuguese territories.

Finding the Money

Since the Casablanca meeting Roberto has left no doubt that he regards himself as the supreme leader so far as Angola is concerned, and has threatened to set up an Angola Government-in-exile in Leopoldville. Whether this threat has caused any misgivings on the part of de Andrade is not known but since it was first made de Andrade has unexpectedly moved his headquarters from Conakry to Leopoldville, leaving da Cruz in Guinea to maintain the necessary liaison. Roberto's financial position also underwent a welcome change after the Casablanca meeting. Immediately before the uprising and for some time afterwards he was hard pressed for funds. His needs were great and urgent – the purchase of rifles and ammunition from Congolese soldiers and, to a lesser extent, from United Nations troops was costly. The French and Belgian Communist parties had given him money but this was soon exhausted when the expected arms from de Andrade did not arrive in time. Appeals to Solod for more money produced unspecified amounts from Moscow, East Germany, Ghana and Guinea, but it was obviously a haphazard way of operating.

After Casablanca it became possible for Roberto to draw on the Afro-Asian Solidarity Fund which had been established in February 1961 at a meeting in Conakry attended by, among others, Solod and Professor B. G. Gafurov, a member of the Presidium of the Soviet Afro-Asian Solidarity Committee and head of the Soviet Commission for Cultural Co-operation.

The fund is administered by a board of which a brother of Sekou Touré, Ismail Touré, is chairman. Board members include Professor Gafurov and a representative of Communist China, Chu Tzu-chi. The fund's charter specifies that it is for the purpose of 'rendering material and financial assistance to any organisation participating in the struggle for national independence, equality, freedom of peoples, democracy and peace and against imperialism and colonialism.'

Although an appeal was made to all member States of the Afro-Asian Solidarity Council for generous contributions to the fund, little more than token payments have been received from most Afro-Asian States. It has been left to Russia and China to finance the fund and the money drawn by Roberto

for his day-to-day operational needs (which still include purchases in the Congo) therefore mainly comes from them. He
claims also to have received financial help from Britain and the
United States.

Roberto has influential friends in the West and he boasts
openly of his links with the American Committee for Africa.
His contact with the United Nations hierarchy in the Congo
is close – so close that during August 1961 he was able to fly
unmolested to Europe in a United Nations aircraft. He was on
his way to attend the Belgrade meeting of neutralist States, but
also took the opportunity to visit London for talks with a few
leading personalities in Britain's political world. Both he and de
Andrade have since visited the United States.

Moscow Has Second Thoughts

At the beginning of 1962 a change in the Soviet attitude
became noticeable. While continuing to laud the 'freedom
fighters' in Angola, there were signs that Russia was making
efforts to extricate herself from any obvious participation in
the Angola bloodshed. Moscow had apparently not foreseen
determined Portuguese military action and had also miscalcu-
lated the reaction of the Africans in Angola.

The two points go together. Solod had accepted assurances
from Roberto and de Andrade that with their first offensive
move a general conflagration would sweep through Angola.
An uprising on a scale which would leave the Portuguese
helpless was predicted and it was taken for granted that
negotiations between Roberto and de Andrade on one side and
Portugal on the other would follow the pattern that had been
set in British, French and Belgian territories.

The fact that by far the majority of Angola Africans
refused to join the uprising and instead flocked to the Portuguese for protecton, thereby eventually confining the area of
revolt to one fairly small region near the Congo border, upset

the prepared plans. This gave the Portuguese authorities a breathing space and the encouragement to meet the uprising with vigour and, as became clear after nine months, considerable preliminary success. According to the Portuguese fewer than one per cent of the Africans in the affected area joined the uprising.

Russia was not prepared for a protracted military commitment in Angola, especially when the outcome in any case began to seem uncertain. Some fresh preparatory work would certainly be needed before there could be a new offensive, and that would take time.

How much breathing space Portugal will now be given is a matter for conjecture. It seems likely that it will be no more than a breathing space because, although Russia withdrew from active participation in the insurrection, there are no signs that Soviet long-term interest in the Portuguese territories is declining.

I have discussed briefly some aspects of the uprising in Angola. I do not return to the subject in the pages that follow. But the above is relevant to the rest of the book because it poses one important question:

How has it happened that Russia, who until 1958 had no standing or foothold anywhere in Africa south of the Sahara, has in so short a time attained a position in which she can exert so much influence in a corner as remote as Angola?

How in fact has the Soviet Union, starting almost from scratch four years ago, become a dominant factor in day-to-day affairs in every part of emerging Africa?

This book is an attempt to give some explanation.

2

MOSCOW DISCOVERS AFRICA

For at least ten years there have been cries of alarm about the Communist danger in Africa. Unfortunately the word Communism is nowhere used more loosely than in Africa and during the past decade it has come to mean little more than purposeful opposition to any existing regime. South Africa set the pattern in this respect, and in doing so has rendered the free world a considerable disservice. Far too often in the past allegations of Communist influence were totally unfounded. The consequence is that warnings of a Communist danger have become debased. Few people will take them seriously any more.

By seeing a Communist plot behind every act of opposition, the self-proclaimed opponents of Communism have in fact done a great deal to facilitate real Communist infiltration, and have contributed considerably towards giving the Soviet Union a status in African eyes which Moscow would have found it difficult to achieve unaided.

The truth is that until 1958 the Soviet Union not only had no organisation working anywhere in Africa south of the Sahara, except the small South African Communist Party, but the Soviet policy-makers were so ignorant about Africa that they were incapable of shaping a coherent policy.

For nearly thirty years the guiding influence on Moscow's attitude towards Africa remained the recommendations drawn up by the Negro Commission appointed in 1922 within the framework of the Communist International. This Commission

saw no difference between American Negroes, the indigenous
peoples of South and Central America, of the West Indies and
of Africa. It recommended one Negro solidarity movement
embracing all these peoples. When, in the nineteen thirties, it
became clear that the Negro Commission's attitude had been
unrealistic, Africa was dropped altogether from the plan.

In the early post-war years Soviet representatives at the
United Nations were unmistakably bewildered when they had
to deal with the problems of the Trust territories, such as Tanganyika, Somalia, Eritrea, Togo, the Camerouns or Ruanda-
Urundi, and Moscow could do little to help them overcome
their ignorance.

In the circumstances the Soviet leaders were no doubt
flattered by the credit they were continuously given for their
great influence in Africa and for their alleged ability to undermine whatever was sound in the Africa which still existed. It
is possible that this is what first induced Russia to take a closer
look at Africa south of the Sahara, but her efforts remained
haphazard until 1957.

It was not until the beginning of that year that it was pointed
out to the Soviet policy-makers, in the words of I.M. Maisky,
at the time head of a commission to supervise the Academy of
Sciences of the U.S.S.R., that 'in the countries of Asia and
Africa truly grandiose events are now taking place. The collapse of the colonial system is going on at such a speed that
the greatest possible effort must be made not to lag behind
life.'

The first sign that Moscow was at last thinking seriously
about Africa came on February 26th, 1957, when what
became known as the Soviet Africanist Co-ordinating Conference was held at the Ethnographical Institute of the Soviet
Academy of Sciences. It was attended by all the African
specialists who could be found, including members of the
Institutes of Ethnography, Oriental Studies, Geography,

World Economic and International Affairs, and by scholars from Moscow and Leningrad research institutes.

One defect immediately became apparent. Only two men at the conference were found ever to have visited Africa.

Professor Ivan Potekhin, of the Academy of Sciences, played a leading part at the conference and his influence on Soviet policy in Africa was to become of the utmost importance. More will be heard of him in the pages that follow.

The main outcome of the conference was a seven-point research plan to study the history of Africa before imperialist partitioning and re-partitioning, the ethnic composition of Africa, the economic situation, the national liberation movements, African geography (natural resources, etc.), and philology. A special study of African languages, with emphasis on Swahili, Hausa and Bantu, was also to be started.

Potekhin gave the order of precedence of the developing Soviet interest in Africa as Algeria, the then French Camerouns, Kenya, Nigeria, Uganda, French West and Equatorial Africa.

Reorganisation at the Soviet Ministry for Foreign Affairs

At that time there was no department in the Soviet Foreign Ministry to deal specifically with African questions. The British colonies in Africa and the Commonwealth countries were the responsibility of the Second European Department, which dealt with Britain. This Department also dabbled in the affairs of countries adjoining British colonies, but as the rest of Africa was the responsibility of the Near and Middle East Department, there was obvious overlapping and serious gaps.

The Soviet approach to Africa remained haphazard until the middle of 1958 when a special African Department was created in the Ministry for Foreign Affairs. First mention of this Department was in July 1958 and its first head was A. V.

Budakov, until then Counsellor of the Soviet Embassy in Prague. A year later he was replaced by A. Shvedov, at one time First Secretary at the Soviet Embassy in Cairo and later head of the North Eastern Department of the Foreign Ministry.

The creation of this Department was an obvious improvement in the organisation, but it still left much to be desired from the Soviet point of view. It immediately became engrossed in the affairs of Algeria and the other countries of the Arab north, and it was only with difficulty that it could cope with the problem of Guinea who, like an orphan child, was dumped on its doorstep late in 1958.

To overcome the inadequacy of the Department and to supplement its work in areas away from the purely Arab north, an African Commission was established at the end of the year. Potekhin was appointed chairman. He brought to the work of the Commission a first-class intellect and drive.

The next important step, taken on Potekhin's initiative, was the establishment of the Soviet-African Friendship Association (in April 1959) of which Potekhin himself became chairman. A few months later an African Research Institute was created, also under the chairmanship of Potekhin.

During 1959 it became clear that Russia was preparing for definite action in Africa. On April 15th, at a meeting of the Soviet Afro-Asian Solidarity Committee, Potekhin said:

'I venture to appeal to all African people to unite . . . Remember in your sacred struggle you are not alone . . . The people of my country, the Soviet Union, have always come out in favour of the right of nations to self-determination and national independence.'

During the same month he wrote (in *Sovremennyi Vostock*):

'Some African leaders, inclined to compromise with the colonisers, assert that the best, if not the only, way to national independence is the way of gradual constitutional reform within the framework of and on the basis of the laws created by the colonisers, the way of negotiations and agreements with the imperialists. Defending the tactic of non-violence, some of them go so far as to condemn in principle the method of violence towards colonisers. But this is a harmful illusion, deliberately fostered by the imperialists in order to prolong their domination of Africa.'

Potekhin pointed out to his superiors in Moscow that there were some basic errors in their thinking. He criticised their assumption that influence could be gained among the new African States by way of Cairo. It was totally wrong, he reasoned, to think that the emerging nations would look to Egypt for leadership. Many more Africans were looking to Ghana. No effort should therefore be spared to establish contact with Accra and friendship with Dr Nkrumah in order to exploit African nationalism.

Potekhin's recommendations were accepted and he was given the responsibility of wooing Ghana, with results that are now known. That Nkrumah's influence has since declined is no reflection on Potekhin's accurate assessment in 1959.

He also urged that intensive study should begin in a new field: the African mentality. Soviet propaganda and activities in Africa should be carefully designed to suit the African's specific mentality. Africans needed a special approach, he said repeatedly, and by the end of 1959 his African Research Institute was asked for recommendations.

The Soviet-African Friendship Association meanwhile grew in importance. One month after it was founded a Guinea-Soviet Friendship Society was organised. This was followed by a Togo-Soviet Committee, a Soviet-Mali Friendship Society (which became, separately, the Soviet-Mali and Soviet-Senegal Societies after the Mali Federation split), and a Soviet-Sudanese Friendship Society. In 1960 and 1961 many more of these societies were formed in almost all parts of Africa, all linked to the parent association headed by Potekhin.

Four Fields of Activity

During 1960 decided progress was made. Potekhin's studies now began to produce detailed blueprints for a concerted diplomatic offensive. In May a report was ready which divided the countries of Africa into four categories, each requiring a different approach. They were: (1) Independent countries (where the emphasis should be on an attempt to influence foreign policy, political alignment and economic policy); (2) Countries on the eve of independence (where possible violence was no longer a practical consideration and where 'front' organisations should become active); (3) Regions where violence was likely and should be encouraged; and (4) Regions where the struggle still lay ahead.

Moscow was still wide of the mark in many respects: two years are not enough to get to know Africa properly. A more profound knowledge of Africa south of the Sahara would have told Potekhin that he had misread the situation in several places. In the third category, for instance, Dahomey, Tanganyika and British Somaliland were mentioned as countries where a violent liberation struggle was to be expected.

The coming troubles in the Federation of Rhodesia and Nyasaland, and the possibility of exploiting them, as well as recurring trouble in Kenya, Uganda and Ruanda-Urundi were, however, foreseen.

The fourth category was hopelessly out of touch with reality. Among the countries where Potekhin thought a bitter struggle still lay ahead were the Ivory Coast, Upper Volta, Niger, Chad, the Central African Republic and the (former French) Congo. This category also included, perhaps more reasonably, Bechuanaland, Basutoland, Swaziland, South-West Africa, the Portuguese territories and French Somaliland.

There is evidence that by now Potekhin had won the ear of Anastas Mikoyan, for many years Russia's Deputy Prime Minister and a powerful voice at the very top. In August 1960, Mikoyan firmly supported Potekhin in his criticism that the studies of Africa then being conducted were too concerned with 'remote topics.' Mikoyan echoed Potekhin's call for the planners 'to come closer to life, closer to modern times, and to link their researches to the tasks of transforming the African peoples' way of life.'

It is of interest to note that an assessment of Soviet prospects in the Congo, prepared on the eve of Congolese independence with the help of the Belgian Communist Party, did not foresee the chaos which was to come. A purely orthodox struggle for Communism to win a foothold and eventually to become a dominant factor in the country's affairs was expected, and a survey made immediately before independence still talked of steps to win the allegiance of the peasantry against the local *bourgeoisie*. Good reasons were found for confidence that the Congo would be transformed into a Communist State. A civil war, although to be exploited if it came, was not expected.

The Second African Department

In 1961 a definite, all-embracing African policy finally emerged. It was in 1961, too, that Russia began to operate with confidence, when her hesitance in the approach to Africa's problems disappeared and when the scales were definitely tipped against the West. Many important changes now took place in Moscow, but the most important for Africa was a further reorganisation at the Soviet Foreign Ministry.

In February the African Department was split into two self-contained departments with equal status. They became known as the First African Department and the Second African Department. Africa north of the Sahara, with special emphasis on the countries of the Maghreb, was made the responsibility of the First African Department, whose head remained A. Shvedov.

The Second African Department was to deal exclusively with Africa south of the Sahara. V. A. Brykin, a career diplomat, until then Counsellor at the Foreign Ministry and previously Chargé d'Affaires at the Soviet Embassy in Belgrade, became its head. For the first time, the Soviet Foreign Ministry had a special Department to deal with what was until then a neglected part of Africa.

Blueprint for Africa

Of only slightly less importance was the adoption of Potekhin's blueprint for Africa, first published late in 1960, as the master plan for Russia's new approach.

I do not intend to discuss dialectics, but it is nevertheless necessary to take a closer look at Potekhin's theories, published under the title *Africa Looks to the Future*, before dealing with actual Soviet methods.

Explaining that Marxism-Leninism suits African conditions in spite of Africa's backwardness, history, social conditions and economic structure, Potekhin nevertheless agrees that Marxist principles will have to be adapted to meet local conditions. For instance, he states that in many cases, where newly-independent States already have 'Socialist-minded' governments (such as Ghana) the 'capitalist stage' of development can be by-passed, just as it had been in Mongolia with the help of the Soviet Government. In any case the transition to Socialism (i.e. Communism) is in his view facilitated by the absence of a significant national *bourgeoisie* and by the fact that the peasant communities often own land on a communal or tribal basis.

(The absence of a significant *bourgeoisie* is explained as due to the inability of Africans to accumulate capital – profits being pocketed by the 'imperialists.')

There are, however, African 'capitalist elements' against whom a class struggle will be necessary. They are in most cases not real capitalists but will conveniently have to take the place of capitalists so that a struggle can be waged against them. The traditional kings and emirs, as found in Nigeria and Uganda, the 'upper aristocratic layers' of the tribes and individual Africans who have entered commerce and have made money are examples of these 'capitalist elements.'

The absence of a significant *bourgeoisie* serves a further purpose, Potekhin believes. Instead of having to marshal the workers against the *bourgeoisie*, the African peasantry, the small working class as represented by the trade unions and the existing *bourgeoisie* (because it is so few in numbers) can all be united in a common struggle against the imperialists. The reorganisation of Africa on truly 'Socialist' lines can therefore go hand-in-hand with the anti-imperialist struggle.

Marxism-Leninism can thus become a 'guiding star' of Africa 'in spite of many contradictions.'

An immediate task, according to Potekhin, must be for the Soviet Union to secure the controlling influence in economic planning, an aim which is now relentlessly pursued in Ghana, Guinea, Mali and Somalia. The 'State sector' of African economies, Potekhin points out, can play an important part in the reorganisation of the way of life of the African peoples.

Potekhin firmly dismisses as unrealistic all talk of an All-African Federation, in spite of the fact that Soviet propaganda pays much lip service to the idea.

Zonal federations, such as that between Ghana, Guinea and Mali, he finds a sounder proposition, but although he appears to think that the Soviet Union should support them whole-heartedly, he seems sceptical about African readiness for such semi-mergers.

On a different plane, Potekhin urges that efforts should be

made to build up an 'African history' and an African cultural background in an attempt to destroy the cultural heritage (he uses the expression 'cultural prison') of the imperialists. In short, what he advocates is a sustained allegation that the colonial Powers destroyed a high African civilisation which, with the help of the Soviet Union, is there for the Africans to regain.

The policy statement which was issued after the Moscow Summit conference of eighty-three Communist parties at the end of 1960, was, though vague, an endorsement of his views. They have since been put into practice.

Four Crucial Phases

Many Soviet 'Africanists,' notably Professor E. Zhukov, head of the Commission for Information and Communication Among African Countries, Professor B. G. Gafurov, head of the Commission for Cultural Co-operation with African Countries, P. Ponomarev and A. Iskenderov, leading party theoreticians, and I. Plyshevsky, *Pravda's* editor for Asian and African affairs and a Foreign Ministry adviser on Africa, have since given more detailed explanations of the basis on which the policy is applied.

It is designed to be carried out in four phases, but one or more can be eliminated where African countries readily accept a 'Socialist outlook.' In short, it allows for improvisation. The four phases are:

1. Independence for any African country is to be encouraged and wholeheartedly supported, irrespective of whether or not that country is disposed towards co-operation with Russia or has inclinations towards 'Socialist thinking.' The only criterion must be that there is a 'bloc of progressive, patriotic forces' struggling for national independence. As an example, support was given to Julius Nyerere in Tanganyika

although he was privately branded in Moscow as 'indecisive' and a 'supporter of the British authorities.'

Zhukov has told 'dogmatists and sectarians' not to sneer at forms of African national movements that do not fit into 'their customary sociological schemes.' He has told them that they are wrong to deny the importance of the formation of independent African States which are led by *'bourgeois nationalists.'*

The formation of any independent State, even if it has *'bourgeois* leaders,' Zhukov has stressed, is of 'great historic importance' in that it is a break-through in the 'imperialist front.'

A. Iskenderov has added an additional explanation, that the 'most active and consistent force' which can be relied on are the workers, even though in many parts of Africa they are still unorganised, 'inexperienced in the class struggle' and with no political organisation. Soviet initiative in the organisation of trade unions for such workers would, however, achieve much, and Iskenderov noted that the formation of an All-African Trade Union Federation was of pressing importance.

P. Ponomarev has added his own explanation. 'A national democracy (in Africa) opens prospects of transition to a higher form of social system.' In any case, by co-operating for a while even with anti-Communist African leaders, the way is prepared for a struggle in each country against 'imperialism and military blocs.'

2. *'Neo-Colonialism.'* Independence for an African State is to be regarded as only the 'first step in the direction of liberation from the colonial yoke.' After liberation must come the struggle against 'neo-colonialism.'

'Neo-colonialism' is defined as the condition in which an otherwise independent African State finds itself if it retains economic links with the capitalist countries or if it accepts economic aid from them. In this connection it should be noted that the 'neo-colonial' Powers are not, in Soviet eyes, so much the former colonial Powers – Britain, France or Belgium – but the United States and, lately, West Germany.

Plyshevsky has explained this aspect of the Soviet attitude thus: 'Most African colonies have achieved formal political independence and more will do so in the near future. Actually, however, the majority of the new African States are still dependent on their former imperial masters. It should be borne in mind that so far it is mainly the political relations between the imperialist Powers and their former colonies that have been affected, while their economic relations in most cases have not undergone any substantial change.

'The old economic bonds have remained as a rule, with the monopolies still holding the key positions. The emergent countries are still within the capitalist international division of labour. Even the political independence of many countries is purely relative.'

Thus, according to Potekhin Nigeria achieved merely internal self-government in October 1960, not independence.

Plyshevsky goes on: 'The struggle for real independence after achieving formal independence is a pressing problem (in Africa) . . . In a number of countries that have won political independence genuine national leaders have come to the fore and are leading the struggle for the achievement of complete independence, both political and economic. Political independence does not signify the end of the struggle against imperialism, but its continuation in new conditions. In some African countries, however, State leadership has passed into the hands of vacillating, conciliatory elements, and even direct agents of the imperialists; here the struggle for real independence will, of course, be fought under more adverse conditions.

'But even in these circumstances, even if their political independence is to a certain extent merely formal, the countries in question have emerged from isolation into the mainstream of world development, wider opportunities have been opened for the growth of the national *bourgeoisie*, and the masses, enriched by the experience of the struggle against imperialism, are spurred on to greater activity.'

Potekhin, the reader will remember, laid it down as an urgent task that the Soviet Union should secure the controlling influence in economic planning in the new States of Africa. The phrase 'neo-colonialism' is an elaboration of this theme and, incidentally, a useful catch-phrase for African nationalists.

A stumbling block for the development of Soviet policy is provided by what Plyshevsky calls 'vacillating conciliatory' African leaders with whom, according to the first phase of the policy, the Soviet Union should nevertheless be willing to co-operate closely.

3. *Leaders to be Deposed*. This, the 'get-tough' phase, which is in every instance to be carefully timed, calls for the ousting of African leaders who resist Communist pressure and who refuse to fight 'neo-colonialism.'

The African leadership to which Moscow objects is not confined to unsatisfactory national leaders. It includes unsatisfactory leadership at all levels where policy or the views of the people can be influenced. Also unacceptable, therefore, are conservative tribal chiefs and elders, who are in many cases the backbone of the community, school teachers or any other Africans of prominence whose outlook has been influenced by Christian or, in some cases, Moslem teaching, African officials who have been trained by the departing colonial Powers and who have retained the principles they acquired under the former system and, of course, political leaders who represent what is regarded in the West as policies of moderation.

But that is not all. Also unacceptable in the long run are genuine African nationalists, however anti-West or anti-European they may be, who insist on a 'hands off Africa' policy. African nationalism itself is unacceptable because its allegiance will at all times be to Africa and not to Moscow. Whereas the West is prepared to come to terms with extreme African nationalism, and has done so in many cases, Moscow cannot do this except as a matter of temporary expediency. Every effort will be made by Moscow to induce such leaders to change their views, but if the efforts fail these leaders will have to go after they have served their immediate purpose.

For the same reason pan-Africanism is also unacceptable to present Communist policy, because if it reflects a genuine sentiment it will give Africa a personality completely removed from Moscow. Potekhin has in fact dismissed pan-Africanism as something not to be fostered seriously.

4. As a last resort, according to policy as now framed, Moscow is prepared to spread chaos in any African country which resists all other methods to induce it to turn towards Russia, or at least to break all links with the West. For this reason control of African trade unions is high on the list of Communist priorities, as will be explained in a later chapter. If necessary the unions will be used to wage a 'Marxist class struggle,' artificially induced, against reluctant leaders.

There are other mass movements apart from the trade unions which are also being prepared for this purpose.

No Role for African Communist Parties

Nowhere in the Soviet policy is there provision for the indoctrination of ordinary Africans. Nowhere is there any mention of the spreading of the Communist faith at this stage among Africans *in Africa*.

The assumption appears to be that by uniting all sections of an African community in a concerted struggle against imperialist oppression and exploitation, which in the Soviet theory does not end after 'apparent' independence, sufficient hostility towards the free world can be induced to prepare the way for the Africans to accept the Soviet liberator. Those Africans who resist this trend will have to be got rid of. That would be a less complicated process than trying to preach Communism at this stage. The only indoctrination which is attempted is among young Africans studying behind the Iron Curtain. But more about that later.

There is also no provision for setting up proper African Communist parties in any country south of the Sahara. It is accepted that the concept of political parties is fundamentally alien to most Africans in spite of the emergence in recent years of various nationalist parties. Potekhin has recommended, and his recommendation has been accepted, that more can be achieved by penetrating existing movements, including trade unions and independence movements.

This method has the additional virtue of overcoming the complication that in South Africa, in the Federation of Rhodesia and Nyasaland, and in most other territories, a Communist Party would not be allowed a legal existence. (The existing South African Communist Party is banned.)

Underground Communist parties would be too difficult to organise in most parts of Africa because of inadequate communications, and because of the high degree of illiteracy among Africans who would mostly be unable to read Communist literature. (There has lately been a slight deviation from this aspect of Soviet policy which is mentioned later.)

Nevertheless, according to Soviet estimates there are today 50,000 active Communists among Africans spread over the countries south of the Sahara, whereas they estimate that there were not more than 5,000 ten years ago. It is not known how these estimates are made or what they are based on, and they are probably totally unreliable. If they are based on assessments made by African Communists, then Moscow still has to learn that estimates made by Africans are invariably inaccurate.

A possible flaw in the Soviet approach may be that it overlooks the Chinese advance into Africa. Russia and China are not marching in step. China is on the move quite independently. It would nevertheless be a mistake for the West to rely on the possibility of a conflict between Moscow and Peking over Africa which would nullify each other's effort. The clash is not likely to be serious enough for that and, if it does take place, is likely to have the effect of spurring each of them on to greater recklessness.

3

PEKING MOVES IN

Although Russian and Chinese activities often overlap in Africa, they are independent of each other and sometimes conflict. It is difficult to assess what the Chinese aim is, other than a pure extension of their belief that world revolution must be encouraged. The Chinese drive in Africa in fact has all the signs of a preparation for revolution and is indeed more reckless than that of the Soviet Union.

The Chinese enjoy many advantages in Africa over the Russians. Being themselves, if not 'coloured,' at least 'non-white' or non-European is by itself a decided asset and makes their motives far less suspect in the eyes of the Africans. As a non-European country, China was, for instance, a full participant in the Bandung Conference of 1955, which Russia could not be. From 1955 onwards China has been accepted as a genuine member of the Afro-Asian bloc and a powerful pursuer of non-European aspirations.

The further fact that China claims to have been herself a victim of 'colonial' or 'imperialist' oppression, and to have thrown off that oppression by her own efforts, gives her a legitimate voice in anti-colonial and anti-imperialist counsels which is recognised by many African leaders. She has, moreover, advice to offer which is based on experience gained in her own 'struggle for national liberation,' and she is not reticent about giving it.

'The experience of China is the summation of experiences, over a long period, in a great number and variety of mass struggles,' Wang Chia-hsiang, of the Politburo Secretariat of the Chinese Communist Party, has declared, adding: 'Naturally, the essence of these experiences is, to a certain extent, of international significance.'

China is, furthermore, an under-developed country, until recently as economically backward as any in Africa, which is making rapid economic and industrial progress since, on gaining 'independence' in 1948-49, she broke what she calls the chains of imperialism. This, in African eyes, is contrasted with the Soviet position – a highly developed industrial country on the European pattern. The Chinese can consequently claim that their methods of development are applicable to African conditions, and many Africans agree with them.

As one Somali put it to me: 'When we visit China we feel at home. When we go to Moscow we see many splendid things, but they are far removed from African realities. They are the same sort of things we see in London or New York. We are simply overawed. In China we can see conditions almost similar to what we have at home, and we can see the progress which we, too, can make by following China's example.'

There is no doubt that Communist China has a fasci- nating effect upon African leaders. The Mali Foreign Minister spoke for many when he said: 'China is advancing at a dizzy pace. Her experience in economic construction is the most remarkable test of the capacity for development of under-developed countries.'

The Chinese message, which is rubbed in day after day, has three simple points: We have a common background (back- wardness and colonial oppression); we have a common enemy (imperialism and colonialism); and, we have a common ambition (national independence and social progress.) Or, to quote the *People's Daily* of Peking: 'The Chinese people, who have gone through a fate similar to that of the African peoples, fully understand and deeply sympathise with the plight of millions of African people under colonial rule and firmly support their heroic struggle for independence and freedom.'

China has one further advantage over the Soviet Union. She need not be inhibited by the need to observe diplomatic niceties. Being in any case a social outcast as far as most Western countries are concerned, and not being a member of the United Nations, she can commit any flagrant breach of political or diplomatic etiquette whenever the occasion calls for it.

Take one example. When the former French Cameroons was being prepared for independence, Russia was for the moment on relatively good terms with France. Immediately independence was attained Moscow furthermore established diplomatic relations with the new Cameroun Government.

But since before independence a Communist-inspired terrorist uprising has been in progress. Moscow has maintained contact with the terrorists, but has had to do so clandestinely, which decreased its effectiveness. China, on the other hand, suffered from no such disadvantage. There was no need for her not to offend President Ahidjo, with whom Peking established no contact. Chinese intervention in the uprising has therefore been most blatant and effective and the subject of open boasting, which has impressed extremist leaders in many parts of Africa.

Much the same happened in Algeria, where Moscow could not maintain official liaison with the F.L.N. and, simultaneously, diplomatic relations with France. China, on the other hand, for long had an Ambassador accredited to the Algerian Government-in-exile.

China's policy towards Africa can therefore be much more dynamic and her association with outright terrorists, including pure thugs and murderers, a matter of pride. It is as well for her that this can be so because the Chinese approach to Africa *is* far more dynamic and considerably more revolutionary than that of Russia. The basic ideological differences between Moscow and Peking and their conflicting views on the pattern of revolution are in fact accurately reflected in their respective approaches.

'War is the Highest Form of Struggle'

In the previous chapter I have briefly explained that Soviet policy calls for initial Russian friendship with all African leaders, no matter how moderate or pro-West they are (the example of the Cameroun Republic is a case in point). This approach is rejected outright by Peking. China will not tolerate moderation.

Neither does the Soviet long-term fear of extreme African nationalism and pan-Africanism apply to Peking. China is confident that her own anti-colonial struggle and her efforts to become less backward have given her so much in common with Africa that she has nothing to fear from the development of a strong African identity or consciousness. The stronger that identity, the closer can be the co-operation between Peking and Africa, according to the Chinese leaders.

It has been argued that one disadvantage for the Chinese is their inability to provide economic aid, or even trade, on a scale likely to make much material difference to new African States. But Peking does not believe in excessive economic aid for Africa, does not believe in what it calls bribery to gain influence there. On the contrary, excessive aid, leading perhaps to relative prosperity, could merely create a conservative middle class not prone to revolution and strong enough to suppress the revolutionary elements.

Where the Chinese find what they regard as really deserving cases, they are nevertheless willing to help. One such case is Guinea, but Guinea has already identified herself sufficiently with China to remove the risk of the aid doing more harm than good.

In general, Russia is prepared to accept a peaceful transition in African States so long as the transition is not too slow, and believes that in most cases African dependence on Moscow can be brought about with proper guidance and help. China rejects this concept: revolutionary wars must be fought; revolution without bloodshed achieves nothing.

'War is the highest form of struggle for settling contradictions between classes, between nations, between States or between political groups,' Mao Tse-tung has written – and his writings are now distributed in great quantities throughout Africa.

Algeria is held up as the example for all 'oppressed' African nations to follow. 'The Algerian struggle for liberation is an important development in the contemporary revolutionary movement in the colonies,' according to Chou En-lai. 'Its influence and significance extend far beyond the confines of Algeria. This struggle has greatly inspired the national and democratic movements in Africa . . . and has become a banner for all oppressed people fighting for liberation. This progressive and just war . . . has set a brilliant example for the national liberation movement of Africa.'

The Chinese leaders even succeeded in presenting the Moscow declaration of December 1960 as supporting their view. The *People's Daily* stated outright that the declaration 'calls on the peoples to rise and fight for the complete elimination of colonialism. It puts forward . . . a fighting programme of carrying to completion the revolutionary struggle for anti-imperialism and anti-feudalism . . .'

Or, to quote General Ho Lung, Deputy Chairman of the State Council and Deputy Chairman of the National Defence Council: 'Standing at the very forefront of the anti-imperialist struggle on the African continent, the Algerian people, with their heroism in waging an unyielding and persistent struggle, have set a brilliant example for the other African peoples in their fight for national independence.'

Many similar quotations can be given. The Chinese are far more outspoken than the Russians in support of extremist African leaders, and their propaganda is blatantly based on what they describe as 'the inevitability of revolutionary action.' Their propaganda also supports extreme economic nationalism, maintaining that political independence is meaningless unless accompanied by nationalisation without compensation of all foreign assets, including banks, railways, and business concerns.

*   *   *

In the view of Peking the liberation of what was French Africa has only just begun. According to China only Guinea has so far attained anything approaching real independence, although Mali is well on the way to it. This is in line with Russian long-term policy, but Peking insists that something be done about it with a minimum of delay.

The 'liberation' of the rest of the former French territories in Africa has been given 'high priority,' according to the *People's Daily*. The 'fight,' it claims, has already started in Cameroun and will have to spread to the rest of West and Equatorial Africa, on the pattern which was set in Indo-China.

North Vietnam as a Model

Repeated reference to Indo-China in Chinese propaganda to the former French territories in Africa is significant, because there is ample evidence that North Vietnam is closely associated with the Chinese plans for this part of Africa. Vietnam, having been a member of the former French Union and having retained much of the French way of life and the use of the language, has a natural link with the States of former French Africa.

Ho Chi Minh, the North Vietnamese leader, was at one time prominent in the affairs of the former French Union, although for long equally prominent in the world Communist movement. He has retained many personal ties with African leaders in former French territories.

North Vietnamese Embassies have been opened in both Guinea and Mali, and North Vietnamese teachers and professors are teaching in Guinea. Significant, too, was the presence of a strong delegation from the North Vietnam General Federation of Trade Unions at the All-African Trade Union Conference held in Casablanca in May 1961. That same month a five-year cultural agreement was signed between North Vietnam and Mali, providing for the exchange of 'information, professors, technicians and journalists.'

A similar agreement has since been concluded between North Vietnam and Guinea. Ho Chi Minh has also established friendly relations with opponents of the regimes in Senegal, Togo and Dahomey, and he was as quick as the Chinese to send an Ambassador to the Communist regime which Antoine Gizenga set up for a time in the Congo's Eastern Province.

Hanoi is now normally included in the itinerary of delegations (of students, trade unions, youth movements as well as politicians – there are now several hundred of them a year) which travel from Africa to China. North Vietnam also has her own Afro-Asian Solidarity Committee which, apart from its links with the former French territories, has established exceptionally close contact with Somalia. North Vietnam has expressed her solidarity with Somalia in a denunciation of the 'imperialists who partitioned Somalia,' and has pledged full support for the Somali people 'in their determination to achieve the early reunification of the country' – i.e. by incorporating part of Kenya's Northern Frontier Province and French Somaliland.

Intervention in Cameroun

To return to the 'liberation' of the former French territories in West and Equatorial Africa, it appears that Peking sees this as a straightforward task: these countries must break all their ties with the West or else their governments must be overthrown by revolutionary movements as soon as possible. It has been made quite clear that Peking's friendship for new African States depends entirely on whether those States adopt policies in line with the militant Chinese form of Communism. Unlike Moscow, Peking does not believe in an interim period of friendship to give the leaders a chance to change their views or allegiance.

An example of this is the insurrection in Cameroun. When the uprising began France was still in control and the aim was stated to be to drive the French out in order to achieve national independence.

But although the fight was ostensibly against the French, the victims were mainly Africans, men, women and children, who were indiscriminately murdered for refusing to join the extremists. Sometimes they were murdered for no other reason than to create unrest.

In January 1960 Cameroun became independent. Free, democratically-conducted elections brought to power a moderate coalition Government led by President Ahidjo.

The terror and bloodshed continued, however. The country was not properly independent, the terrorists claimed, because it was led by French stooges. The civil war dragged on, seemingly without end. According to Chinese doctrine, the Government had to be replaced by a truly revolutionary body. Just how deeply involved China had become in the insurrection became evident with revelation that groups of terrorists from Cameroun were receiving military training in China. (China, it should be pointed out, only appeared on the scene in Cameroun at a fairly late stage – see chapter nine.)

The disclosure came when six men were arrested. Papers found on them and information they gave during questioning established that they had just completed an intensive ten-week course of training in sabotage, guerrilla warfare and political subversion in China. They had left Cameroun without travel documents in March 1961 and had been taken by air to Peking.

The training, at a military academy outside the capital, included instruction in the manufacture of explosives, the use of mines and grenades, surprise attacks and ambushes, the destruction of barricades and the capture of sentries, the fortification of villages, the destruction of bridges and the sabotaging of airfields, railways, telephone lines and other means of communication.

Another phase of the training was devoted to political study, with lectures on Communist ideology. The course, it was subsequently discovered, was the fourth of a series for young Africans from Cameroun. It has since been found that courses for Africans from other territories are also conducted, the aim being to produce an adequate supply of African guerrilla leaders who are then returned to their respective countries to become both rebel leaders and Chinese agents.

Recruits from Nigeria, Uganda, Kenya, Tanganyika, Nyasaland, Rhodesia and the Portuguese territories, in addition to those from former French territories and Algeria, have attended the courses.

The Sino-Russian Clash in the Congo

Chinese readiness to aid what they regard as the right kind of African movement was also shown in the Congo. On August 25th, 1960, the Chinese Ambassador in Cairo, Chan Hiang-kang, arrived in Leopoldville as an observer at a pan-African conference which had been convened by the late

Patrice Lumumba. His arrival coincided with a torrent of propaganda from Peking praising Lumumba for having adopted the correct policy, particularly in defying the United Nations. Documents exchanged at that time between Chan Hiang-kang and the Lumumba faction have since been published, and their authenticity has not been denied by Peking.

For example, on September 8th, Gizenga, then Lumumba's Deputy Prime Minister, handed Chan Hiang-kang a letter addressed to the Chinese Government asking for details of the help China could give by making available volunteers, arms, ammunition, fighter aircraft, helicopters, tanks and armoured cars, money and food.

The Chinese reply was given four days later. It read in part: 'The Government of China and the Chinese people support the Government of the Congo and the Congolese people against the intervention of the imperialists headed by the United States under cover of the flag of the United Nations. The struggle is grandiose and just . . . The Chinese Government is quite willing to do all it possibly can to give assistance to the Government of the Congo, but considering the relative geographic position of the Congo and of China, it is difficult to send military volunteers.

'However, the Government of China has decided, in the first place, to offer foreign exchange to the Congo. It is sending its first aid of one million pounds, which it places at the Government's disposal. As to other aid requested, in particular means of transport, the Government of China is in the course of studying the problem . . . '

The letter was signed by Chan Hiang-kang.

That the promised aid (apart from the money) was in the end withheld because of the sudden eclipse of Lumumba does not detract from China's willingness to intervene. Later, when Gizenga set up a separate State in the eastern Congo, Chinese attempts to send supplies were frustrated by the Sudan's refusal to allow transit facilities.

China's interest in the Congo provided an example of a direct clash with Russia.

The gulf between them first became apparent when Peking Radio bitterly criticised the United Nations' decision to send a military force to the Congo, in spite of the fact that Russia had voted in favour and strongly supported the resolution. Shortly afterwards, when the Soviet Union demanded increased powers for the United Nations contingent, Peking denounced its presence as a violation of Congo sovereignty and called on the Congolese to wage an 'heroic struggle' against the U.N.

A second serious divergence became public in August 1961, when a new central Government was set up with M. Adoula as Prime Minister. Gizenga, in Stanleyville, recognised this Government and agreed to serve in it as Deputy Prime Minister. Simultaneously he acknowledged that he had ceased to be the head of a sovereign government (the one he had established in Stanleyville). Russia expressed tentative approval and Khrushchev sent a message to Adoula conveying his best wishes for success in strengthening the Congo's independence and unity.

Peking, on the other hand, immediately denounced Adoula as a Western stooge, refused to recognise his Government and continued its recognition of Gizenga, ignoring the fact that Gizenga had nominally joined the Adoula Government. Subsequently, the Chinese Ambassador who had been accredited to the Stanleyville Government was withdrawn altogether; he could not be transferred to Leopoldville as the Leopoldville regime had recognised Nationalist China a year previously.

Even after that, however, Peking continued to refer to Gizenga's non-existing government as the only 'lawful government.'

The Advance

Communist China's concern with African affairs began, so far as can be known, in 1955. That was the year of the Afro-Asian conference at Bandung at which African affairs were discussed at length. It is likely that until that time China was not aware just how vulnerable Africa was, or of Africa's potential usefulness in preparating for world revolution. But China lacked direct contact with Africa.

The first opportunity to remedy this came the following year, with the Suez crisis. President Nasser's appeal for all possible help against Britain and France was immediately answered by expressions of solidarity from Peking. Diplomatic relations between the two followed and China opened an Embassy in Cairo.

The Embassy became for a while China's forward base in Africa. One of the tasks Chan Hiang-kang, the Ambassador, concentrated on was the establishment of trade relations with African countries; another was the use of the Afro-Asian People's Solidarity Council to make direct contact with African leaders from as many parts of Africa as possible. The Council's permanent headquarters was in Cairo, and China was a member.

Chan Hiang-kang did a first-class job. During 1957 he established trade relations with the Sudan, Libya, Tunisia, Morocco, Nigeria, Ghana, Ethiopia and even with Tanganyika, far to the south. Friendly relations with many of the leaders also became possible.

Invitations to visit China were freely extended, and during the next twelve months thirty-one delegations from twenty-one African countries were entertained in China and taken on extended tours through the country. During that same period seventeen Chinese delegations paid return visits to African countries. One result was that China won diplomatic recognition from the Sudan, Morocco, Ghana, Guinea and Tunisia.

By 1959 Chinese Embassies had been opened in Khartoum and Rabat, and China's advance into Africa was on its way. Peking Radio started its powerful daily broadcasts beamed to all parts of Africa, transmitted in excellent English, French, Swahili, Arabic and, later, also in Portuguese. By the end of 1961 ninety-one hours a week were devoted to these broadcasts. Through the diplomatic missions excellent, well-produced propaganda literature has been distributed since 1959 in ever-increasing quantities.

The Influx of Embassies

Nineteen-sixty was the real turning point. As had happened two years previously in Moscow, proper organisations were now set up in Peking to deal with Africa. A slight set-back was Nasser's cooling-off towards China. This severely handicapped work from Cairo, but experience was to show that Guinea is a better bridgehead than Egypt, and since 1960 the Chinese Embassy in Conakry (opened early in that year) has in fact been the main base of operations.

China, who had no diplomatic missions anywhere in Africa until the end of 1956, today has twelve Embassies, several lesser missions operating vaguely in 'West Africa,' 'East Africa' or 'North Africa,' and countless technical, economic, cultural and other missions scattered through a large part of the continent.

There are today in fact more Chinese Embassies in Africa than on any other continent (including Asia), and there is closer contact with Africa than with most of Asia. The Embassies (at the beginning of 1962) are in Egypt, the Sudan, Ethiopia, Somalia, Libya, Tunisia, Morocco, Mali, Guinea, Ghana and, on and off, the Congo, as well as the Embassy accredited to the provisional Algerian Government.

And that is referring only to official Chinese representation, not to unofficial contacts which have been established with the terrorist movements in Cameroun and lately in Angola, with the Uganda African National Congress, the Kenya African National Union (whose Vice-President, Oginga Odinga, was given a standing ovation at a rally in Peking when he described the 'glorious and heroic Mau Mau' who had saved Kenya), the Tanganyika African National Congress (whose President, Zùberi Mtemvu, described the 'misery suffered by the Tanganyika people under the imperialists' during a speech at a banquet in his honour in Peking), the Zanzibar Nationalist Party, Nyasaland's Malawi Congress Party, and others too numerous to list here.

Significantly, only two Embassies have been opened in former French West and Equatorial Africa – in Guinea and Mali. The other governments in these two former French regions are earmarked for liquidation, and their friendship therefore is not worth cultivating.

The Channels of Control

Four main organisations, whose activities are co-ordinated and whose membership often overlaps, guide China's activities in Africa. They are:

1. The Chinese Institute for African Affairs. (Established in September 1960.) Its director, Ny Yung-chen, is a member of the Central Committee of the Chinese Communist Party.

2. The National Afro-Asian Solidarity Committee. (Established in April 1960.) The chairman, Liao Cheng-chih, is also first secretary of the Overseas Operations Department of the Chinese Communist Party.

3. The China-Africa Peoples' Friendship Society. (Established in April 1960.) Although vaguely modelled on its Soviet counterpart, it has an entirely separate existence. Its director, Liu Chang-sheng, a member of the Central Committee of the Chinese Communist Party, is also deputy chairman of the All-China Federation of Trade Unions.

4. The Special Committee on Relations with Peoples of Africa. This committee appears to be simultaneously a Government, party and military organisation and its activities seem to be under the direction of Li Keh-nu, formerly head of the Social Affairs (Secret Operations) Department of the Chinese Communist Party.

Li Keh-nu is also head of the organisation co-ordinating the work of these four committees. Its Chinese name can best be translated as the Special Work-Toward-Africa Committee. Liu Chang-sheng is its secretary-general.

Many Chinese missions have toured various parts of Africa, but the crucial mission was led by Liu Chang-sheng himself. Accompanied by eleven other key persons all holding senior appointments in one or more of the four organisations listed above, he toured Guinea, Mali, Ghana, the Niger Republic, Togo, Dahomey, Upper Volta, Ethiopia and Somalia from March to July 1961.

On his return to Peking Liu Chang-sheng announced that it had become clear to him that 'the African people have come to understand that the imperialism of the United States is their most vicious and dangerous enemy.' He added: 'The fighting friendship of the African people for the Chinese people is today indestructible by any imperialist force . . . The need now is to establish a broad national united front against imperialism.'

Liu Chang-sheng's findings and recommendations were at the end of 1961 accepted as the basis on which a 'forward-looking' Chinese policy for Africa was to be worked out.

Peking is more secretive in its ways than Moscow, but a few recent signs indicate that it has been decided that East and southern Africa can benefit from closer Chinese attention. Chinese support for the 'struggle against new constitutional proposals for Northern Rhodesia' (expressed by cable on August 21st, 1961) is one such indication; another is an expression of support (by the National Afro-Asian Solidarity Committee) for the 'people of Nyasaland in their national struggle;' yet another is a declaration by the All-China Federation of Trade Unions expressing solidarity with the South African Congress of Trade Unions.

'Mutual solidarity' between China and the Zanzibar Nationalist Party (which emerged as the biggest party in the election of 1961) is on record. So is lavish entertainment extended in Peking to trade union delegations from Angola, Nyasaland, the Rhodesias, Uganda, Zanzibar and Tanganyika.

Zanzibar is being prepared as the jumping-off place for East Africa and possibly also for southern Africa, with Ali Sultan Issa of the Zanzibar Federation of Progressive Trade Unions (and a member of the Zanzibar Nationalist Party) as China's main agent for East Africa. In 1961, Ali Sultan Issa received comprehensive training in trade union organisation in China, and one of his tasks at present is to recruit students from the East African territories for study in China.

Africa the Loser

A considerable part of the Chinese effort in Africa is to warn against the alleged imperialist threat which now comes from the United States. 'Neo-colonialism,' on the Moscow propaganda pattern, is a repeated charge against America.

'In Africa, American imperialism is ceaselessly intensifying its activities in order to grab colonies and extend its sphere of influence,' is an example of the propaganda theme. So, also, is the charge that 'U.S. imperialism, which is trying to replace the older colonialists, is being recognised by more and more Africans as a dangerous enemy of their freedom and independence.'

In Somalia the theme has already won recognition. Abubakar Sucoro, chairman of the Somali National League, and Mohammed Mohad, chairman of the Independence Constitution Party, while on a joint visit to Peking in 1961, publicly endorsed the view that 'U.S. imperialism remains the biggest threat to the Asian and African peoples and they are fully aware of this.'

Since 1960 the number of African students studying in China has increased steadily. No figures are available, but in April 1961, there were enough of them to form a 'Union of African Students in China' with Elias Okidi of Uganda as President and E. John Hevi of Ghana as secretary-general. The aims of the union were announced as 'fostering co-operation and unity among African students struggling for the total liberation of Africa from colonialism and neo-colonialism, and ousting imperialism from Africa and the whole world.'

Details of the steady flow of persons – students, trade unionists, political leaders, cultural 'experts' and others – now travelling weekly between all parts of Africa and Peking can be given, but this is not intended as a detailed chronicle of the day-to-day relations between China and Africa. It is an effort merely to give an indication of the trend and the increasing momentum of China's drive.

There are many indications that the Soviet Union is uneasy about the rapid strides China is making. But this uneasiness is part of the bigger conflict between the two Communist giants; it does not affect the basic aim they are both pursuing in Africa.

In any case, the rift between China and Russia as far as their respective African policies are concerned is not deep enough to give Africa a breathing space. Fundamentally, the difference of opinion is merely whether Africa can be won by the deceptive means in which Russia believes, or whether a bloody revolution must be accepted as desirable and inevitable.

Either way, Africa will be the loser if the Africans are abandoned by the free world.

4

THE ECONOMIC OFFENSIVE

'The problems facing the nations which have just recently gained their freedom make it imperative for them
to broaden economic co-operation with the Socialist
countries. This co-operation is now becoming one of the
decisive conditions of national regeneration and genuine
independence for the former colonies and semi-colonies.'

World Marxist Review (June 1961)

The Russians maintain, rightly, that the free world's
strongest anti-Communist weapon in Africa is the economic
dependence of the emerging countries on the West. It follows
that the ending of that dependence has a high priority in the
Russian scheme.

According to A. Kutsenkov, one of the main architects of
Russia's economic offensive in Africa, 'the main effort of most
of the nations of Africa which have won national independence is shifting to the sphere of economy. It is here that
colonialism is making a last-ditch stand, clinging with
particular tenacity to its position.'

And: 'In the final analysis, the success of the struggle for
freedom and independence in the former colonies will depend
on whether the healthy forces in these nations are able to break
the resistance of the reactionaries and imperialism, effect broad
social and economic reforms . . . and thus open the way for
the development of the productive forces.'

An outline of the Soviet economic aims in Africa, prepared
jointly by Kutsenkov and D. Degtyar, deputy chairman of the

State Committee for Economic Relations until his appointment in January, 1962, as Soviet Ambassador to Guinea in succession to Solod, says bluntly: 'The extension of relations with the Socialist (i.e. Communist) camp helps the patriotic forces of these countries to cope speedily and successfully with their national problems.'

Russia's economic drive in Africa is not, however, purely for political gain. Many envious references have been made to Africa as a source of raw materials which the Communist countries badly need but which now go to Western countries.

For instance, writing about the 'imperialist plunder of Africa,' I. Plyshevsky says: 'What does Africa mean to the imperialists? Basic raw materials for the industries of the capitalist countries – copper, uranium ore, cobalt, manganese ore, iron ore, oil, tin, gold and diamonds, as well as rubber, cotton, coffee, cocoa, oil-bearing nuts and other products. The enormous mineral resources, still far from fully surveyed, the advantageous location of many of the deposits, the cheap labour power and the possibility of using forced and even slave labour – all this makes Africa a particularly coveted prize for the monopolies.'

This has been the subject of a special study which appeared in Moscow in May 1961 under the title of 'Raw Material Resources in Africa During the General Crisis of Capitalism.' Its appearance coincided with a Polish proposal that a Soviet bloc 'investment credit pool' be set up to help 'underdeveloped countries to produce the raw materials in which the Soviet bloc countries are interested' and a Hungarian plea that arrangements be made for 'more and more' raw materials.

Africa is Still 'Capitalist'

The Communist economic drive in Africa began to make progress only during 1960. Earlier overtures ended disappointingly for the Russians, as they have admitted on a number of occasions. But having carefully analysed their earlier failure they believe they have discovered the reasons.

Basically they have found an immense handicap in the fact that former colonial territories remain, of necessity, economically linked to their erstwhile motherlands and generally have economic systems which have been introduced by 'capitalist countries.' Exploration and development, for instance, are still largely in the hands of private enterprise. Mines producing valuable minerals are mostly owned and operated by Western companies who consequently have full control over the disposal of raw materials.

Poland, for example, has found that she has to buy 90 per cent of the minerals she imports from Africa through London, Paris or Rotterdam. 'The dominating position of highly-developed capitalistic countries in the markets of under-developed countries is still a fact which must be seriously reckoned with,' a survey on the subject states. Moreover, due to the non-Communist structure of the economies in Africa, the governments of those countries are 'not as free as they would like to be to enter into unrestricted economic relations with Socialist countries.'

For the Soviet aid programme to have the desired effect various changes will therefore have to be engineered in African countries, according to the survey. Africans will have to be persuaded to go over to 'planned' economies, and private or 'capitalist' enterprises and assets will have to be nationalised. With the demand for nationalisation, Soviet interest therefore neatly coincides with extreme African nationalistic aspirations, a fact that has been noted in Moscow with satisfaction. The problem has accordingly been reduced to a simple formula: 'The struggle for *real independence* after achieving formal independence is a pressing problem . . . for African countries.' (The italics are not mine but those of Plyshevsky.)

Unfulfilled Promises

Many of the Soviet bloc's sweeping offers of aid to African countries were, incidentally, extended before Moscow had examined the difficulties. When the implications of the analysis became clear, much of the earlier promised aid did not materialise. More than half of the 970 million dollars' worth which had been promised to various African countries by the end of 1960 has never been delivered.

On the other hand, African countries which have gone over to a so-called planned economy and have shown proper enterprise by beginning to nationalise foreign assets, such as Ghana and Guinea, have received everything they had been promised.

In spite of all the publicity the Soviet bloc contrives to get out of every offer it makes (whether fulfilled or not), Communist aid is so far minute when compared with Western aid. By the middle of 1961 the Soviet bloc's aid programme for all under-developed countries taken together, spread by then over eight years, came to the equivalent of 4,000 million dollars. United States aid alone for the single year 1959-60 came to 2,860 million dollars. Add to this the fact that more than half of the Soviet bloc aid promised was not in fact delivered, and the difference becomes considerably greater.

Nevertheless, better propaganda apart, the Soviet bloc has some decided advantages over the West in exploiting any aid given. First, Soviet aid goes only to carefully selected targets. Whereas American aid, for example, goes to almost every spot between Formosa and Latin America, Moscow selects targets with only one consideration in mind: how will the aid further Soviet interests. American aid, by being so widely spread, loses the impact of concentration.

Second, Soviet aid is always given for projects which are politically popular and therefore coincide with nationalistic aspirations, such as the Aswan High Dam in Egypt or the hydro-electric power project in Ghana.

Third, wherever possible the West keeps a careful check on how its aid is used, the assistance being intended to bring genuine help to poorer nations and not wealth to a few individuals. This supervision often leads to resentment, not only on the part of some African politicians who would like to pocket a large slice of the aid. It offends even honest Africans who detect in Western scrupulousness a slight to their nationalistic feelings.

Soviet aid, on the other hand, is given for its political impact and if it all disappears into the pockets of a few leading African politicans it is not all that important so long as those politicians can be considered bought. In any case, all the propaganda value will have been obtained from the aid before its disappearance into private pockets.

Fourth, the Soviet bloc (in this case including China) can offer one incentive for the development of secondary industries in Africa which the West cannot do: it can offer to import consumer goods. However crude or inferior those consumer goods may be, there is a ready sale for them not only in China but in Budapest, Bucharest, Warsaw and in many parts of the Soviet Union.

Soviet Bloc 'Experts'

Fifth, no Western country can compare with the Communist bloc in exploiting the African need for technical experts. If a technician is needed for a particular job in Africa, the Western country concerned tries to find a man who knows something about the subject. In the administration of aid, or in efforts to develop trade, the West is therefore inclined to send economists, businessmen or technicians who are wholly untrained in the political complexities of Africa. International agencies, such as the World Bank, do the same.

The Communist bloc, in contrast, ensures that every 'expert' sent to Africa is a highly-trained man, not necessarily in the subject on which he is alleged to be an authority but in the special task he is to perform in Africa for the Communist cause. Early in 1961 Moscow claimed that more than 6,000 Soviet bloc experts were in former colonies, and that there would be more than 12,000 by the end of 1962. More than half of the 6,000 are believed to be in African territories, and more than half of the promised 12,000 can be expected to be in Africa by the end of 1962.

These men work as a team, under central direction from Moscow, irrespective of whether they happen to be Czechs or Poles or Hungarians and they know precisely why they are there and what is expected of them. In contrast, 'experts' from the United States, Britain, West Germany or from the various United Nations agencies not only work to no central plan (there being none) but they are far too often in conflict with each other, in direct competition or simply falling over each other's feet. All too often they spend much of their time undoing each other's work.

Russia is, moreover, careful not to alarm young African countries by sending too many *Russians*. Czechs, East Germans, Poles and others serve the purpose just as well and ensure that there is not too great a concentration of Russians in evidence.

Special organisations now exist in most of the Iron Curtain countries to train and provide the specialists where and when needed. In Poland, to give one example, an 'Office for Providing Technical Services Abroad' was set up in May 1961. Known for short as the *Polservice*, it gave special training to 200 men selected for foreign service during the first seven months of its existence.

The Soviet Case Against the West

The never-ending allegations of 'neo-colonialism' against the Western Powers, and particularly against the United

States, is part of the effort to discredit both Western aid and the Western advisers and technicians serving in Africa. The theme is simple: African States who accept Western aid and Western 'experts' surrender part of their independence to a new form of colonialism.

'There is a fundamental difference between the co-operation of the Socialist States with the economically under-developed countries and the relations existing within the capitalist world economy, where the strong oppress the weak, the rich rob the poor, where anarchy prevails and the economic relations between nations are constantly being disrupted,' according to Kutsenkov. 'In the Socialist countries the working people hold the reins of government and their relations with other countries are naturally free from exploitation and enslavement and are permeated with the spirit of genuine equality and friendship.

'The Socialist States have no interest in seizing foreign markets. They supply other countries only with the commodities that are not produced by the industry of the country concerned. This makes for the fuller and broader utilisation of the national wealth and resources of the economically backward countries.

'Unlike the imperialist monopolies, the Socialist States do not demand any share in the profits or in the administration of the enterprises built with their assistance. Hence the credits extended by the Socialist countries have nothing in common with the export of capital. The relations of the Socialist countries are free of any taint of haggling or profit-making.'

The Soviet case against the West is, in contrast, indeed painted black for the African leaders. I quote Plyshevsky (writing in July 1961) at some length. I have not attempted to correct his figures.

'The British, French, U.S., Belgian and West German monopolies have made huge investments in African countries and are garnering enormous profits there. The capital of the British companies incorporated in the Federation of Rhodesia and Nyasaland totalled £20,200,000 at the end of 1956, and their annual dividends exceeded £10 million. The annual profit of some of the mining companies operating in Northern Rhodesia has run in some years to more than 200 per cent on the invested capital.

'In the Congo, the capital of the *Union Minière du Katanga* stood at 5,000 million francs in 1950. As a result of further investment, financed mainly by ploughing back some of the profits, its net return increased from 600 million francs in 1946 to 4,500 million in 1959 . . .

'Since the end of the Second World War the U.S. monopolies have been steadily increasing their African investments. According to incomplete data, the U.S. State and private capital in Africa now exceeds 2,000 million dollars. Recent years have also witnessed the penetration of West German capital into this quarter of the world. Although their investments are not very high as yet (172 million marks), the West German monopolies, now exceedingly active, are increasing their share in the plunder of the African peoples.

'Imperialist investments since the Second World War have mostly gone into expanding basic mining operations. In the period from 1940-50 to 1955-57 the extraction of manganese ore increased by 36 per cent, chromium 45 per cent, copper 55 per cent, asbestos 64 per cent, iron ore 88 per cent, cobalt 96 per cent, lead 113 per cent, zinc 124 per cent and bauxite by 304 per cent.

'African oil output in 1960 exceeded 10 million tons, and by 1962 the Sahara alone is expected to yield more than 20 million tons. The proportion of African mineral raw materials to the total consumed by the industries of the capitalist countries is increasing year after year.'

According to Plyshevsky's figures (which are for 1956)

C

African copper accounts for 24 per cent of the free world's total consumption, manganese ore for 37 per cent, tin ore for 15 per cent, antimony for 48 per cent, gold for 63 per cent, and cobalt for 80 per cent. He then goes on:

'The foreign trade of the African countries is almost wholly controlled by the monopolies of the principal imperialist countries . . . Most of them (the African countries) are still raw material producing adjuncts of the industrial capitalist Powers – sources of raw materials and agricultural and forest products.

'Non-equivalent trade is the salient feature of the commercial relations between the capitalist monopolies and the African as well as other under-developed countries . . . Non-equivalent trade is a form of plundering the economically under-developed countries which, increasingly, get smaller quantities of industrial goods from the capitalist countries in exchange for their raw materials. Besides, raw material exporters have been hard hit by the decline in the world market prices of raw materials.

'The foregoing explains the tenacity with which the imperialist powers are striving to hold the African countries in subjugation . . . They will not readily give up the fabulous profits they are squeezing out of Africa or hand over to its people the vast natural resources that supply them with raw materials.'

'Western Aid is a Trap'

I do not know to whom Plyshevsky primarily addressed these words. The extracts are taken from the *World Marxist Review*. It can, however, be accepted that it is part of the 'message' which the several thousand Soviet 'experts' are spreading in Africa, as well as the teaching given to African students in the countries behind the Iron Curtain.

Mr Kenneth Kaunda, leader of the Northern Rhodesian

United National Independence Party, for instance, has often said that the British South Africa Company's activities were a main obstacle to African aspirations. It has similarly been repeatedly claimed that 'foreign financial interests' are working against African nationalism in Katanga and in the Portuguese territories. Moscow Radio, in broadcasts to Africa, has attributed Britain's 'cynical refusal' of African demands to the 'reluctance of British business to abandon its interests in Northern Rhodesia.'

But Plyshevsky's words are more than a message to Africa. They are an argument directed at the Soviet leaders themselves, telling them of the fabulous wealth which is today within easy reach, urging them not to lose sight of this valuable prize, and adding for good measure what a blow it will be to the free world if the West is driven out of Africa altogether.

I am not making any attempt here to answer Plyshevsky's indictment. That is a separate subject outside the scope of this book.

In Communist bloc dealings with Africa it is repeatedly alleged that the 'capitalist' countries are determined to prevent the industrialisation of the young African States. Western aid is portrayed as a trap to ensure that industrialisation is kept to a minimum. It is claimed that the Communist bloc, on the other hand, while not attempting to impose industrialisation on anyone, is at all times ready to assist it 'in deference to the wishes of their partners.'

The former U.S. Secretary of State, Mr Christian Herter, is conveniently quoted as admitting that a feature of Communist aid is the obvious desire to promote projects in which the under-developed countries are themselves interested.

Another argument attractive to emerging Africa has been outlined by Kutsenkov and Degtyar. I quote them: 'With their traditional branches of industry and agriculture constantly at the mercy of the periodic slumps in the imperialist States, they (the under-developed countries) find the prices of their commodities slashed and part of the burden of the crisis thus shifted to their shoulders.

'Technological progress in the capitalist countries is replacing' many types of agricultural and other raw materials by synthetic products with resultant shrinkage in the market for the traditional exports of the under-developed countries.

'In the period between 1928 and 1955-57, world industrial production rose by 146 per cent, while the exports of the under-developed countries (not counting oil) increased by only 23 per cent. Development of the new branches of industry is retarded by the restricted home market – the result of the general economic backwardness and foreign monopoly competition.

'In these circumstances, trade with the Socialist States acquires particular importance for the economically under-developed countries. By giving them a market for the sale of their produce it enables them to increase production and to obtain the additional financial and material means necessary to spur their development.

'As distinct from the imperialist monopolies, the Socialist States do not confine their purchases in these countries to the traditional exports – raw materials, fuel, food products; they also buy the products of the new national industries, thereby stimulating their growth and helping them to revise the structure of their economy.'

A feature of Soviet bloc credits granted to African States is that there is usually provision for repayment in raw materials. Or, as Russian propaganda explains it: 'Payment on Soviet loans is made as a rule by deliveries of staple products, a system which obviates the need for the recipient countries to look for foreign currency, ensures them a market for their commodities and at the same time serves to expand those branches of industry and agriculture in which they specialise. This helps to increase employment and to raise the living standard of the local population.'

Soviet Prospecting in Africa

Communist bloc 'experts' are available to help recipient countries to search for raw materials with which to repay credits and loans. By agreement, for example, more than a hundred Soviet geologists are in Guinea, prospecting for gold, diamonds and what is officially referred to as building materials. The operation of many existing mining installations in Guinea has been taken over by Russian engineers and by the end of 1961 extensive Soviet laboratories for geological research were being built in the country. In this way the Russians are being repaid at least part of the 70 million dollar loan made to Sekou Touré.

Soviet prospectors have begun similar operations in Mali. Russia has in fact given Mali a loan to pay for the prospecting operations.

Soviet geologists have also started a survey of the northern region of Somalia. Suitable raw materials, if found, will go to the Soviet bloc to pay for Russian agricultural machinery, industrial equipment and manufactured goods. Soviet prospecting is also in progress in Ethiopia and may start soon in the Sudan.

Russia is not likely, however, to reveal what her geologists find and there is little the West can do to keep a record.

The Soviet mistake of dumping unwanted raw materials to deflate world prices is not likely to be repeated. In earlier years, before Russian policy had been clearly laid down, that happened sometimes.

Both Russia and Czechoslovakia, for example, received great quantities of cotton from Egypt during the years 1957-59. They immediately resold much of it on Western markets at deflated prices, thereby seriously damaging Egypt's trade. Another example was Indian sugar. In 1961 India was desperately trying to persuade the United States to take 600,000 tons of her sugar; Communist countries which had bought her sugar the previous year had dumped large quantities of it on her traditional Asian markets.

These were errors of judgement not likely to be repeated, except as a punitive measure if an under-developed country steps out of line. There is even a suspicion that in the case of the Egyptian cotton the dumping was done deliberately to bring Nasser to heel.

Control of Economic Planning

Getting hold of Africa's raw materials, however, remains a secondary aim. A more important target is to get control over economic planning in Africa.

Three years ago this would have seemed an impossible task for any Russian to set himself. The economic structures built by the West seemed too deeply entrenched to be in danger of a complete overthrow. Since then time and events have shown how over-optimistic that belief was.

Guinea is admittedly an exceptional case, having been abandoned, destitute, by France and left in no position to refuse any conditions Russia imposed on her in return for immediate help. Nevertheless, the fact cannot be ignored that Guinea's present economic development plan has been worked out for her entirely by Communist bloc advisers, nor can the further fact that 85 per cent of the capital needed to carry out the plan is being made available by Russia and satellite countries.

In addition, Communist bloc advisers have accepted full responsibility for supervising the implementation of the plan. The quarrel between Sekou Touré and the Russian Ambassador, Solod, which led to Solod's expulsion, does not alter the picture.

Whatever reservation may be felt in Ghana about such complete acceptance of Soviet guidance, economic integration between Ghana and Guinea is Nkrumah's declared aim. That means the adoption of at least a similar type of planned economy for Ghana. Early in 1962 Nkrumah accordingly scrapped his current Five-year Plan and asked for Soviet advice in drawing up a Seven-year Plan to replace it.

The Mali Government has formally and voluntarily approached the Czech Government with a request that the Czech National Committee for Planning and Economic Management should in future supervise the drafting and execution of all Mali's economic plans. According to *Ceteka*, the official Czech news agency, this was agreed to in accordance with the Soviet bloc's 'deep desire to be of help to young African countries.'

Somalia appears to waver between accepting economic advice from Czechoslovakia, Hungary, Russia or China. She has not yet made a final decision, but her intentions are clear.

If Nyasaland should become independent both of Britain and the Federation of Nyasaland and Rhodesia, Dr Banda's intention to ask for Russian economic assistance and advisors is on record.

An independent Zanzibar governed by the Left-wing Zanzibar Nationalist Party cannot be expected even to want to resist Soviet bloc advisers for long, especially if the Communist bloc countries should discover that they are suddenly in need of cloves, Zanzibar's main but declining export. And in Kenya the demand for a 'socialised economy' on the Soviet pattern has already started.

Sea Communications With Africa

That the Soviet bloc is confident of achieving a tremendous increase in its export-import trade with Africa is placed beyond doubt by its strenuous efforts to organise adequate shipping facilities between Communist ports and Africa.

In 1959, when the flow of goods between Guinea and Communist countries first started, a serious handicap was the lack of the Soviet bloc's sea communications with West Africa. It was an embarrassment to have to rely on free world shipping which could make cargoes subject to scrutiny. In any case, it made the shipment of military equipment difficult if not impossible.

At the end of 1959 a special new shipping line was therefore formed under the Polish flag to ply between Conakry and Communist ports.

Called the *Polska Zegluga Morska*, this line began operating with one smallish ship which carried 50,000 tons during the first twelve months. At the end of 1960 the two-way flow of goods between Communist and West African ports began to increase rapidly and a second ship had to be chartered.

By mid-1961 the volume of trade (and aid) had grown to such an extent that four further ships, two of 10,000 tons each and two of 6,000 tons, had to be added to the *Polska Zegluga Morska's* fleet. Estimates made by the line's headquarters in Warsaw predicted that more than 500,000 tons of cargo would be carried by these ships before the end of 1961. Further additions to the fleet were planned for 1962, when a continued increase in the traffic was predicted.

During 1961 the Soviet Union, finding it no longer convenient or necessary to rely so much on Polish shipping, began to send an increasing number of her own ships to African ports.

It is difficult to assess the volume of Soviet bloc trade with Africa. The young African countries seldom publish figures. Sometimes the information is deliberately withheld, but more often they simply do not have the necessary machinery for collecting and analysing statistics. Russia normally prefers to refer to percentages which do not convey much when it is not known on what they are based. To talk, for example, of a 114 per cent increase in trade between the Soviet Union and Africa within a given period, which is what Russia does, is meaningless.

Nevertheless, the enlargement of the shipping line and the recent addition of Russian ships to this service leave no doubt that the growth must be exceptional, even allowing for the fact that three years ago it started from almost nothing. It does not, of course, compare with the volume of Western trade, but to feel reassured for the future by that would be too optimistic.

Credits to be Increased

A last word should be said about credits. Soviet bloc credits, vague and misleading as the statistics concerning them are (an estimated 500 to 700 million dollars' worth have so far been granted to African countries), are normally repayable over a period of twelve years. Interest terms are extremely low.

A warning that the amount of credits is to be sharply increased has been given by Professor Lazlo Hay, rector of the Budapest Karl Marx University. Paradoxically, the warning was addressed to the members of the *Comecon* countries. (*Comecon* is the Soviet bloc's council for mutual economic assistance.)

In July 1961 he warned the satellite countries that great as their needs for Soviet credits are, they will in future have to rely on their own financial resources because Soviet credits will henceforth go mainly to former colonial territories and to countries fighting for independence.

It should once more be stressed that until 1959 the Communist bloc had no economic link with any part of Africa south of the Sahara. The progress made therefore represents the work of only slightly more than two years, during a period when East Africa (Kenya, Uganda, Zanzibar and, until December 1961, Tanganyika) was under British control, making it impossible for those countries to succumb. The same thing applies to Rhodesia, Nyasaland, the Portuguese territories and, for different reasons, to South Africa.

5

OF TOILERS...
(African Trade Unions)

Professor Potekhin and others have stressed their belief that Africa's present small working class will grow and that, if properly organised, it can be turned into a 'vital force in the anti-imperialist struggle.' According to Iskenderov the workers can become 'the most active and consistent force in the liberation struggle.'

The regimentation of African trade unions is more important for Moscow than getting control of any other non-Communist trade unions because in Africa Communist parties as such either do not exist or are ineffective. In any case this policy fits in with the Soviet acceptance that ordinary political parties are still alien to almost all of emerging black Africa.

The World Federation of Trade Unions (W.F.T.U.) was from the outset the front organisation used to ensnare willing and unwilling African trade unionists. Formed in 1945 as a non-political international organisation, it was rejected by all non-Communist trade union organisations four years later. The West's trade unions formed, instead, the International Confederation of Free Trade Unions. The W.F.T.U. headquarters is in Prague. All trade unions in the Soviet bloc are affiliated to it.

The First Steps

In 1959 Moscow decided that one central all-African trade union association or federation affiliated to the W.F.T.U.

would be easier to control than a number of separate trade union movements scattered all over emerging Africa. From that time on the W.F.T.U. has ceaselessly preached the need for an all-African trade union federation.

One reason for Moscow's decision was that the International Confederation of Free Trade Unions (I.C.F.T.U.) was winning the support of many individual African unions: twenty-two in fact became affiliated to it. Bitter attacks on the I.C.F.T.U., with all Communist propaganda media in Africa branding it as an imperialist tool, failed to shake the loyalty of those twenty-two unions: the I.C.F.T.U.'s influence actually seemed to be growing.

The Communist demand was therefore suddenly changed. What was really wanted, Moscow decided at the beginning of 1960, was an all-African trade union movement ostensibly not affiliated to *any* international organisation 'so as not to hamper its work for the protection of African workers.'

Africa's biggest Communist labour organisation, the *Union Générale des Travailleurs d'Afrique Noire* (U.G.T.A.N.), active throughout former French West Africa, dutifully disaffiliated from the W.F.T.U., a move which received wide publicity. An effort was then made to build this organisation up as a nucleus for an all-African trade union federation.

But the plan did not work. Guinea's estrangement from many of the other former French territories seriously weakened the U.G.T.A.N., whose headquarters is in Conakry, and, in addition, there appeared to be an unbridgeable gap between the trade union movements in former French Africa and the trade unions in British, or former British, territories.

Luck, however, favoured the Communist efforts. In 1958 the first All-African Peoples' Conference (a non-governmental group sponsored by Nkrumah) had met in Accra and Abdoulaye Diallo, a leading U.G.T.A.N. official and a former

W.F.T.U. Vice-President, had been elected as that organisation's secretary-general. The following year Ghana's Trade Union Congress had broken with the I.C.F.T.U., leaving it unaffiliated to any international labour movement.

This was an ideal situation, especially as pan-Africanism is one of Nkrumah's dreams. When Russia decided on a new approach it did not take Abdoulaye Diallo long to persuade Nkrumah to let the Ghana Trade Union Congress become a sponsor of the all-African trade union federation concept.

The full weight of the Nkrumah-sponsored All-African Peoples' Conference was now also given to the project, and in January 1960 an 'executive secretariat' was set up to make preparations for the establishment of an all-African trade union movement.

The 'executive secretariat' consisted of a Moroccan President and six secretaries, four of whom had been trained by the W.F.T.U. A W.F.T.U. secretary, Ibrahim Zacharia (a Sudanese living in exile and who is in charge of the W.F.T.U.'s African affairs) was retained, unofficially, to help with the work.

The project immediately received the formal approval of the W.F.T.U., whose General Council passed a resolution that the steps taken would make a great contribution to the 'liquidation of colonialism.'

But the going was not to be smooth. A number of African trade unionists remained to be coerced.

Two important stumbling blocks were the Tunisian trade unions who were affiliated to the I.C.F.T.U., and who valued the affiliation, and Tom Mboya, leader of the Kenya Federation of Labour and a Vice-President of the I.C.F.T.U., who has been practically hand-fed by the American A.F.L.-C.I.O. and whose finances depend to a considerable extent upon retaining American goodwill. The Liberians, also affiliated to the I.C.F.T.U., showed resentment too.

Mboya, while supporting an all-African movement in principle, advocated freedom for each individual member organisation to decide on its own affiliation with international organisations. He was supported by the Tunisian unions, but as the Ghana-Guinea faction, backed by the W.F.T.U., refused to alter its attitude the first preparatory meeting, held in Tunisia, came to nothing. A further preparatory meeting in Lagos also failed to produce agreement.

Deception and Dishonesty in Casablanca

The 'executive secretariat,' spurred on by the W.F.T.U., decided not to wait any longer. It was by now already well into 1961 and more than eighteen months had been wasted. Besides, with more delay the initiative might pass to non-Communist movements. An inaugural conference was therefore convened, to take place in Casablanca in May 1961.

The Casablanca conference did finally produce an All-African Trade Union Federation (A.A.T.U.F.) of sorts, but only by means of blatant Communist trickery and deception and a show of determination which should be a warning to all Africa that Communist regimentation of the trade unions is going to be ruthlessly carried through. Some anti-Communist African trade unionists were deeply alarmed by what happened, but they were unable to stem the tide.

The Casablanca conference was attended by eighty-seven delegates from thirty-five African trade union organisations and by eighty-two observers, including Alexander Bulgakov, secretary of the Soviet Central Trade Union Council, and a Chinese delegation.

A W.F.T.U. delegation brought a message from its secretary-general, Louis Saillant, that the W.F.T.U. 'approved in principle the setting up of a united African centre to express the wishes and claims of African workers,' which would intensify the struggle against the 'remnants of colonialism' and the 'attempts to introduce neo-colonialism to Africa.' Messages of goodwill and solidarity were received from Khrushchev, Chou En-lai and a host of other Communist leaders.

All those who attended, delegates and observers alike, had been invited by a preparatory committee which had taken great care to ensure a majority in support of the draft proposals. The delegate invited from Uganda was John Reich, who was described as President of the Uganda Federation of Labour, an organisation which exists only on paper. The Uganda Trade Union Congress was not invited. On its own initiative it sent a delegation which challenged John Reich's status and successfully proved that he did not represent a single trade union or worker.

Liberia, whose trade unions have close links with the I.C.F.T.U., was not invited to send delegates; only observers. The three 'observers' who did turn up, representing Liberia's Congress of Industrial Organisations, therefore displayed cards saying 'Liberia is in Africa' and demanded to be accepted as delegates. The Pan-African and Malagasy Union of Christian Workers, which had been ignored, hurriedly met in Brazzaville and sent a strong protest to Casablanca.

This accused the sponsors of the Casablanca conference of having invited only selected organisations, some of which were 'unrepresentative, minority and splinter movements,' and a few entirely bogus delegates. A similar protest came from Morocco's massive *Union Générale des Travailleurs de Maroc* (U.G.T.M.) which had not been invited although the smaller *Union Marocaine du Travail* was one of the sponsors.

Ahmed Tlili, secretary-general of Tunisia's *Union Générale Tunisienne du Travail* complained bitterly that most of the delegates were selected fellow-travellers and included Africans who had no contact with any trade unions, some of them in fact living in Communist bloc countries.

This view was supported by a Nigerian, Lawrence Borha,

of the Trade Union Congress of Nigeria, who said: 'What threatens this conference is dishonesty – those who shout at the top of their voices for positive neutrality and do not say that when they leave this hall they will go to Moscow.' Tom Mboya of the Kenya Federation of Labour denounced Communist activity behind the scenes.

But these, and many more, protests did not unnerve the W.F.T.U. – supported sponsors who steam-rollered their way through the conference. They had appointed a steering committee before the conference began, they avoided having standing orders, there was no credentials committee and no voting procedure. Decisions were taken by 'acclamation,' which made it possible for the organisers to swamp the hall with *Union Marocaine du Travail* members, who were obediently in attendance, whenever necessary.

'Total War' Threat

The issue was not whether an all-African trade union federation was desirable or not. Nearly all African trade unions support the idea in principle. The issue was whether member organisations of such a federation should have the right to maintain contact with the I.C.F.T.U. and whether individual unions should have the right to have Western affiliations.

Theoretically the issue was equally whether any links should be maintained with the W.F.T.U. But the W.F.T.U. had encouraged non-affiliation – the all-African body was to be riddled with W.F.T.U. stooges, to make affiliation unnecessary – thereby making contact with the West the only matter in dispute.

Many genuine delegates strongly defended the right of any trade union organisation to be affiliated to whichever international body it wished. The extremists, however, refused to give ground and it was soon clear that the proceedings were so rigged that any moderate voice could be drowned.

In disgust a number of delegations walked out, refusing to attend the final session when the charter was to be adopted. They included those from the Kenya Federation of Labour, the Trade Union Congress of Nigeria, and the *Union Générale Tunisienne du Travail.*

Even so, the issue was never put to a vote: the Charter was adopted by acclamation. All member unions who were affiliated to any international organisation were given ten months to end the affiliation. In other words, all African trade unions were given ten months to sever their ties with labour movements in the free world.

If any refuse to do so, 'total war' will be waged against them, according to John Tettegah, secretary-general of the Ghana Trade Union Congress who was appointed a secretary of the all-African federation. 'We shall isolate them,' he said, 'and enter their countries and form A.A.T.U.F. unions there. It is as simple as that – total war.'

The extent to which the W.F.T.U. retained control can be seen from the fact that the A.A.T.U.F. secretariat consists of eight members of whom seven were W.F.T.U.-sponsored secretaries of the preparatory committee. The eighth is Tom Mboya who was elected in his absence after he had left the conference.

The reason for his election is obvious. It will give the A.A.T.F.U. an oportunity to penetrate East Africa, and it was in fact decided to set up a regional secretariat in Nairobi. Other regional secretariats are to be in Accra, Cairo, Bamako and Conakry. The organisation's headquarters is in Casablanca. The President is Mahjoub ben Seddick of the *Union Marocaine du Travail.*

Moscow's 'Deep Gratitude'

Moscow had reason to be pleased. In 'Africa Looks to the Future' Potekhin had written (with reference to the great need for an all-African trade union movement which could be placed under Communist domination): 'However, the schismatic activities of I.C.F.T.U. agents of the reformist trade unions of Britain and France create difficulties which it has not yet been possible to overcome.'

During the conference Moscow Radio had said that the I.C.F.T.U. 'is trying to ensure economic and political privileges for the Western monopolies in Africa' by insisting that affiliation of African trade unions to international trade union organisations be allowed. I.C.F.T.U. was described as the 'yellow trade union international.'

After the Casablanca conference Moscow Radio announced that the 'principal task' which now lay ahead of the A.A.T.U.F. was 'to intensify the struggle against colonialism.'

Trud, quoted by Moscow Radio, expressed complete satisfaction with the outcome 'in spite of the intrigues of U.S. trade unionists and the so-called I.C.F.T.U.' Alexander Bulgakov, secretary of the Soviet Central Trade Union Council who had led the Russian delegation to Casablanca, visited Ghana immediately afterwards. There he expressed 'deep gratitude to the Ghana movement for the successful laying of an unshakable foundation for the A.A.T.U.F.'

He added: 'Tettegah (secretary-general of the Ghana T.U.C.) and other African nationalists should be commended for their ability to stand against the I.C.F.T.U.' After the Casablanca conference Tettegah travelled to Moscow to discuss closer co-operation between Soviet and Ghanaian trade unions.

Ibrahim Zacharia, the Sudanese secretary of the W.F.T.U. in charge of its African operations, followed with a call to all African trade unions to join the A.A.T.U.F. and urged the formation of 'workers' cadres' to intensify the 'struggle against colonialism.'

The W.F.T.U., meeting in Moscow, expressed 'solidarity

with the A.A.T.U.F. in the struggle for the liquidation of colonialism,' and Moscow Radio commented: 'It is clear that the active participation of the African trade union organisations will be of great importance for the abolition of the colonial system.'

But many Africans were far from happy. A typical comment representing moderate opinion was made by the Nigerian *Daily Times* of Lagos: 'The Casablanca All-African Trade Union Conference was a failure . . . The extraneous issue of international affiliation raised at the conference by the Ghana, Guinea and Mali faction was politically inspired and not industrially or economically. It is dishonest, negative, dictatorial.

'No trade union in Africa has had the moral courage to declare officially and openly its affiliation to the Communist-controlled World Federation of Trade Unions, but it has been clear all along that some trade unions are in secret alliance with that organisation. On the other hand, there are twenty-two trade unions that are officially and openly affiliated to the International Confederation of Free Trade Unions, which is the workers' own international organisation; democratic, independent and free from employer or government control throughout the free world.'

The Tunisian *Neo-Destour* newspaper, *Al Amal,* said the conference had failed because it had been diverted from its original purpose of creating a pan-African trade union organisation based on reason and legitimacy and turned into a collection of different blocs having suspect aims.

Mr Henshaw, acting general secretary of the Trade Union Congress of Nigeria, also claiming that the conference was a failure, added that the decisions were not taken by the genuine representatives of African trade unions but by 'splinter groups, individuals representing nobody, and hired hooligans.'

The Tunisian trade union leader, Ahmed Tlili, stated

bluntly that his union, the *Union Générale Tunisienne du Travail*, would not consider itself bound by the conference resolution on disaffiliation.

Tlili did in fact make an effort to organise a rival, non-Communist federation based on Dakar, but without success. The Casablanca organisation, in spite of the strong opposition to it, has had a flying start. Although further attempts will be made by moderate unions to minimise its importance, the fact that the W.F.T.U.-sponsored All-African Trade Union Federation now exists, with a declared policy of fighting Western interests, is a new factor in African political life which cannot be overlooked.

Many moderate Africans who were encouraged by Tom Mboya's initial denunciation of the Casablanca movement were soon discouraged by his lack of action against it. His failure to renounce his election to the secretariat disappointed many. His further agreement that a regional secretariat could be established in Nairobi seems to have ended his active resistance to the A.A.T.U.F.

Many unions have refused to break their links with the I.C.F.T.U. and have not joined the A.A.T.U.F., but the pressure against them is formidable. How long they will be able to hold out is uncertain. What is not in doubt is that Moscow today has an invaluable tool in the A.A.T.U.F. which places almost every African worker indirectly within its reach, and which enables it to exert influence in almost every town and city in Africa. It has provided Russia with one of her main weapons.

The I.C.F.T.U. appears to have been hopelessly outmanoeuvred; the W.F.T.U. leaders certainly were far more adept in handling African trade unionists than the leaders of the I.C.F.T.U. For this the American A.F.L.-C.I.O., as the dominant influence in the I.C.F.T.U., must bear a large share of the blame.

Training for African Trade Unionists

While the W.F.T.U. is the principal channel for contact between the Communist bloc and African unions, it is by no means the only link. Direct contact between African and Communist bloc unions is increasing rapidly. Training in trade union organisation is one of the main baits, and East Germany, in this as in other forms of education, plays a particularly important role.

The W.F.T.U.'s training of African trade union officials started in Budapest in August 1959, with a series of four-week courses. From the outset the courses were mainly political, the admitted intention being to emphasise the 'struggle against colonialism and the role of the African trade unions in the fight for independence.' The first course was attended by thirty selected union leaders from ten African countries, including Guinea, Senegal, Cameroun, Congo and Madagascar.

These courses still continue, but Budapest was found to be rather remote and since the beginning of 1960 East Germany has overshadowed Hungary in this respect. The first mention of East German activity came at the end of 1959 when *Tass* reported that 200 Africans drawn from eighteen nations were attending a conference in Leipzig sponsored by the W.F.T.U.

No further details were given; in fact, every effort was afterwards made to keep the conference secret and it is assumed that the *Tass* report was an indiscretion.

The next important step was taken nine months later when the Leipzig Trade Union College opened a special institute for foreign study. The opening ceremony, conducted by Herr Warnke, President of the East German Trade Union Federation, was attended by seventy African trade union officials from Ghana, Guinea, the Congo, Nigeria, Somalia, Togo, Cameroun, Zanzibar, Ivory Coast, Angola, Morocco and Algeria.

They were reported to be on an eight-month course conducted in English and French. The institute will eventually be able to accept 300 African trade union officials at a time.

In his opening speech Warnke said that African workers would find their true friends in East Germany and other countries of the Communist bloc. As part of the policy of extending friendship to African workers, the East German unions were providing training facilities for 'many' African trade unionists, Warnke continued, as well as supporting Algerian patriots and generally helping African trade unions to establish and develop themselves.

The institute, he added, would help to 'train African trade union cadres,' instructing them in trade union organisation and helping them to acquire the 'scientific outlook of the working class.' It would at the same time enable Africans to 'prepare themselves for the anti-colonial struggle.'

Three months later (in December) the East German Trade Union Federation announced that it had given more than £250,000 (at the official rate of exchange) to trade unions in Ghana, Guinea, Senegal, Nigeria and the Ivory Coast, part of the money being earmarked for trade union schools.

In April 1961 it was further disclosed that the East German trade unions had given 100,000 Guinean francs to the trade union school of the *Union Générale des Travailleurs d'Afrique Noire* (U.G.T.A.N.) in Conakry. The East German Federation was also to present the U.G.T.A.N. with a printing house.

During the same month an agreement was concluded between the East German Trade Union Federation and the Nigerian Trade Union Congress providing for close co-operation. (The Nigerian T.U.C. must not be confused with the Trade Union Congress of Nigeria. The Nigerian T.U.C. is a Communist splinter movement representing thirty-three unions. The T.U.C. of Nigeria, which is anti-Communist, represents about ninety unions.)

Similar agreements have been signed with Guinean,

Ghanaian, Malian, Somali, Togoan, Camerounian and other African unions, and hardly a week passes without the arrival of an African trade union delegation being reported in East Germany.

Among the other satellite countries, Czechoslovakia is also becoming important as a training centre for African trade union officials. During 1960 formal ties were established between a number of Czech trade unions in Ghana, Nigeria, Senegal, Cameroun and Algeria, and in June of that year it was announced that the Czech Central Council of Trade Unions had opened a centre for African trade unionists to study political and economic subjects. The centre is at Jiloviste, near Prague. The courses last ten weeks.

In 1961 special courses for African trade union officials were also introduced in Poland and Bulgaria.

Russia herself is playing host to an increasing number of African trade union leaders who are invariably given V.I.P. treatment. Tashkent, capital of Uzbekistan, is now used as a centre for seminars to which they are invited. During 1961 trade unionists from Ghana, Guinea, Zanzibar, Mali, Somalia, Kenya, the Congo, Cameroun and Uganda attended study groups held there.

During 1961 Moscow Radio, in broadcasts to Africa, began to devote much time to African trade union affairs. The theme is blunt and direct: the time has come for African workers to organise themselves in a broad national democratic front and to strengthen their ties with 'anti-imperialist' trade unions who are ready to help them in their quest for freedom and independence.

Since its formation the A.A.T.U.F. has passed many resolutions, every one of them relating to outright political rather than trade union affairs. Typical was one in support of Soviet policy regarding a peace treaty for Germany, conveyed to an East German trade union conference held in September 1961, which was attended by a number of African trade union officials. The A.A.T.U.F. has similarly expressed approval of the Soviet Communist Party programme of September 1961.

The A.A.T.U.F. appears to waste little time in dealing with what in the West would be regarded as trade union matters, such as wages and working conditions. When it is not busy with its campaign against the West, its efforts are directed against moderate non-Communist African leaders, or trade unions who value their association with the I.C.F.T.U.

6

. . . AND TERMITES
(Front Organisations)

Although some spectacular Communist successes have been achieved in several countries, the slow, steady sapping away of Africa's vitality is taking place away from the public eye. The almost imperceptible subversion which is constantly taking place, against which there is almost no defence, may eventually be much more telling.

Moscow, understandably, prefers not to be seen directing the subversion. Front organisations are used, in most cases the same front organisations which are active in Western Countries. If it is taken into consideration that even in sophisticated countries such as Britain, France, Italy or the United States the influence of, for instance, the World Federation of Trade Unions or the Women's International Democratic Federation has caused concern, then it will be understood that these organisations can be exceptionally effective in unsophisticated and often uncritical African countries.

The front organisations in all cases ostensibly pursue policies which cannot fail to appeal to Africans, and they all have the outward appearance of being non-political, non-partisan and non-official. In every case, however, full control is in the hands of a small select group of Communists whose election is not subject to popular vote.

The international front organisations fall into three main groups: trade and professional, women and youth, and semi-political, peace and solidarity movements. In all cases they are

instruments of Soviet policy and can operate without the help
of an organised local Communist movement.

Not all the international front organisations have been
successful in Africa; those that have made no significant
impact are not discussed here. The success of the World
Federation of Trade Unions, the Women's International
Democratic Federation, the International Union of Students,
the International Organisation of Journalists (in association
with the International Radio and Television Organisation), the
World Federation of Democratic Youth and the Afro-Asian
Peoples' Solidarity Council have, however, been exceptional.

The work of the World Federation of Trade Unions has
already been discussed in the previous chapter. Of the remaining organisations the Afro-Asian People's Solidarity Council
has attracted most attention in recent years, but is by no means
the most sinister. Many African leaders are fully aware of its
purpose.

The Solidarity Movements

The Afro-Asian Peoples' Solidarity Council (A.A.P.S.C.),
created in December 1957, must not be confused with the
Afro-Asian conference at governmental level which was
convened by the Colombo Powers in 1955 in Bandung.
Strenuous Soviet efforts to dominate the Bandung Conference
failed dismally and ended with Russia not even allowed to
participate.

Soviet failure at Bandung was, however, the direct reason
for setting up the A.A.P.S.C., and Russia claims persistently
that it is the descendant of the Bandung gathering. This is not
so. Heads of States and Heads of Governments participated at
Bandung and decided on a policy of non-alignment. The
A.A.P.S.C., on the other hand, consists mainly of representatives of extremist movements, many of them in exile, seeking
alignment with Russia.

With permanent headquarters in Cairo, it has affiliated to it committees for Afro-Asian solidarity representing a number of countries, including a Soviet Committee for Afro-Asian Solidarity, a Chinese Committee for Afro-Asian Solidarity, a Guinean Committee, a Malian Committee, a Ghanaian Committee, a Somali Committee, and so on. But some of these committees do not function from the countries which they claim to represent. They are, instead, based on Cairo, in exile.

One of the Solidarity movement's declared aims is to fight not only colonialism but, even more strenuously, 'neo-colonialism,' especially American neo-colonialism. Another aim is to extend the political, economic and cultural influence of Russia (and China) in Africa.

Only a few full meetings of the A.A.P.S.C. have been held. On each occasion Soviet bloc representatives far outnumbered African delegates.

The resolutions which have been passed on these occasions are revealing. One has called on African governments to nationalise foreign capital without compensation and to make a distinction between 'disinterested aid from friendly, anti-imperialist countries' and imperialist aid whose aim is to keep Afro-Asian countries as a source of cheap raw materials. The World Bank has been denounced as an instrument of imperialist exploitation, and close co-operation has been urged with countries which have a 'planned economy,' especially the Soviet Union.

The usefulness of the A.A.P.S.C. to Russia was demonstrated in October 1960. To coincide with Khrushchev's appearance at the United Nations in New York when he made his anti-colonialist declaration, the Soviet Afro-Asian Solidarity Committee called a conference in Stalinabad, the capital of Tadzhikistan, to debate 'The Peoples of Africa and Asia in the struggle against colonialism and imperialism and the activity of the Soviet Afro-Asian Committee.'

Representatives from many African countries were invited, but most of the delegations consisted of African students from Soviet universities. The conference dutifully endorsed Khrushchev's declaration and called for the 'stepping up of the struggle for the immediate and final destruction of colonial regimes.'

The picture conveyed to the world, and particularly to Africans, was one of complete identity of interests and views between Khrushchev and Africa, with Khrushchev championing the African cause on the international scene. That it was an erroneous picture was unimportant. Many African nationalists were impressed.

Financing Subversion

An important development came in February 1961, when the Afro-Asian Solidarity Fund was set up. The decision to establish the fund was taken at a meeting in Conakry attended by Soviet delegates including Gafurov of the Soviet Afro-Asian Committee.

An appeal was made to 'all progressive organisations fighting against colonialism and imperialism' to contribute to it, and, as already mentioned, the purpose of the fund was given as 'to render material and financial assistance to organisations participating in the struggle for national independence, equality, freedom of peoples, for democracy and peace, and against imperialism and colonialism.'

The administration of the fund is confidential, but it is a useful instrument through which Russia can supply large quantities of money to African organisations without the funds being traceable back to Moscow. Even Africans who would hesitate to accept Russian money have no qualms about accepting it from a so-called Afro-Asian solidarity movement.

It has been established that the fund has been a great help to the terrorist leaders in Angola. Gizenga, while in Stanleyville, also received generous amounts. So, too, have the terrorist leaders in Cameroun and some of the money has found its way to Kenya, to be used by Oginga Odinga for the Kenya African National Union. Northern Rhodesia's United National Independence Party has also already derived benefit.

The A.A.P.S.C. does, however, suffer from two weaknesses, both becoming apparent only fairly recently. One is that both Russia and China are represented on the permanent controlling body in Cairo. With the divergence of Russian and Chinese activities in Africa as a result of their separate policies, the secretary-general, Yusuf as-Sibai, an Egyptian, has to serve two masters. This causes some lack of coherence and decrease in effectiveness.

The other is that Nasser's friendship with China, and even with Russia, is no longer as wholehearted as it was when the A.A.P.S.C. was created. As host to the permanent headquarters he can have a dampening influence and there have been several suggestions that the headquarters should be moved to Guinea. This has so far been resisted by Egypt, but a 'regional bureau,' which is beginning to overshadow the main headquarters in importance, has been set up in Conakry.

The Conakry office also provides the much-needed liaison with the All-African Peoples' Conference, the non-governmental body established under Nkrumah's auspices and which has its permanent headquarters in Accra.

Previously the link between the two organisations was difficult to maintain in view of some jealousy between Nkrumah and Nasser. Now, with Nasser's influence in the A.A.P.S.C. declining, Nkrumah's attitude has changed. There is now closer co-ordination and *Tass*, the Soviet news agency, has commented on the Accra-based movement's 'new higher stage in rallying the Africans.' *Izvestiya* has also noted that the Accra body has become 'more specific and more militant.'

The A.A.P.S.C. at least makes no effort to disguise its

hostility to the West and its obvious adherence to the Communist cause. It is therefore to some extent possible to keep a check on what it is doing. This is not so in the case with most of the other front organisations active in Africa.

Journalists Under Control

The International Organisation of Journalists (I.O.J.) is an example.

Formed in June 1946 at a congress in Copenhagen, the I.O.J. was intended to replace the pre-war International Federation of Journalists. By 1950 control had so obviously passed to Communist representatives that all non-Communist associations broke away to re-establish the International Federation of Journalists. Most of the I.O.J. members today are therefore from the Soviet bloc, and one of its objects now is to oppose 'every form of journalistic activity in the service of individuals or groups whose interests do not coincide with those of the working masses.'

I.O.J.'s secretary-general, Jiri Meisner, is foreign editor of the official Czech newspaper, *Rude Pravo,* and its senior Vice-President is D. F. Kraminov, vice-chairman of the Union of Soviet Journalists. The headquarters is in Prague.

In October 1960 the I.O.J. sponsored an 'international' conference in Baden, Austria, where Communist bloc journalists played host to invited delegates from African countries, notably from the former French territories. One of the conference decisions was that an 'African Committee' should be formed to co-operate with the I.O.J. The Africans present formed the committee on the spot, under the leadership of a Senegalese, Doudou Gueye, a former member of the French Communist Party.

When the African delegates left Baden they had undertaken to convene an all-African conference of journalists.

Subsequently, early in 1961, Doudou Gueye toured Eastern

Europe and Russia as guest of the I.O.J. According to the I.O.J. journal, *Democratic Journalist*, he was given valuable help and guidance on how to set about establishing an all-African journalist union. He was also given help in convening the promised all-African conference of journalists, which was eventually held in Bamako in May 1961.

One of the main items on the conference agenda was 'The problems of the Press in Africa, its role in the struggle against colonialism and its relations with international Press organisations.'

African journalists from Ghana, Guinea, Upper Volta, Zanzibar, Mali, Algeria and Cameroun attended, but they were outnumbered two to one by delegates from Russia, Czechoslovakia, East Germany, Poland, Hungary, Outer Mongolia and China. One delegation represented the I.O.J. and another the International Radio and Television Organisation (O.I.R.T.), whose headquarters is also in Prague. Doudou Gueye presided.

The delegates from behind the Iron Curtain undertook to provide scholarships for African journalists to study in Eastern Europe, to exchange 'experts' and technicians to help the Press of young African countries, to provide and install printing presses where necessary and to give all possible help to establish African information and Press agencies.

The most important outcome of the conference was, however, the unanimous decision to establish the All-African Journalist Union (U.J.A., from its French initials). Jean Deen, editor of the Guinea newspaper, *Horoya*, was elected President and Doudou Gueye became secretary-general.

According to a conference decision, the U.J.A. would be allowed to maintain relations with other journalistic bodies, but only if these were 'democratic journalists' organisations' with 'progressive' aims.

The objects of the U.J.A. were given as: To help in the

struggle for the liberation of Africa and against neo-colonialism, to fight against nuclear tests and racial discrimination, to work for African unity, and to seek support for both the Afro-Asian Peoples' Solidarity Council and the All-African Peoples' Conference as well as for the All-African Trade Union Federation. It was also agreed that an all-African news agency, a 'Voice of Africa' radio station and an all-African school of journalism should be established as soon as possible.

Many of Africa's best-known and most able journalists were not at the conference and have not joined the U.J.A. But they are now up against a well-organised movement and their work will become difficult as the I.O.J.'s offshoot gains influence.

Although the U.J.A. was established only in May 1961, it is receiving such expert help and guidance that a great deal has been achieved in the short time that has elapsed. Significantly, too, Western news agencies have since been denounced as 'tools of imperialism' and an appeal has been made to African journalists to examine all Western Press reports carefully and sceptically before making use of them.

Training for African Journalists

At the request of the I.O.J. the East German Journalists' Association has appealed for 'solidarity' with Africa and has undertaken to make scholarships available to African journalists. A public savings account has been set up for the purpose and it is claimed that so many contributions are coming from all over the country that it will also be possible to buy printing equipment for African States. The Dresden branch, acting on its own, established an African Solidarity Committee and collected £8,000 which was spent on printing equipment for Mali 'as a token of fraternal aid.'

Meanwhile Czechoslovakia and Poland have jointly opened a school for journalists in Conakry and the East German

Journalists' Association has undertaken to co-operate with the Czechs in opening a school in Bamako. The Czech Ministry of Information has signed an agreement under which the official Czech news agency, *Ceteka*, has set up a news agency for Mali, and Bulgaria has undertaken to train journalists from Ghana, Guinea and Mali in 'modern newspaper production.'

Russia also has not been backward in offering help, and the first batch of journalists from Mali, Togo and Cameroun arrived in the Soviet Union in August 1961 to be trained under the guidance of the Union of Soviet Journalists.

By the end of 1961 the I.O.J. had consolidated its entry into Africa, and the influence of the U.J.A. was beginning to be felt by African journalists as far south as Tanganyika and Rhodesia.

Again, it is not that Britain and France, or even the United States, have not done a great deal to train African journalists. It is merely that the Communist bloc has tackled the problem differently, through an effective front organisation. As a result much of the West's effort to impart sound journalistic standards is being nullified.

The activities of the International Radio and Television Organisation can be linked with those of the I.O.J. Founded in its present form at a meeting in Helsinki, the intention was to create a link at professional level between employee organisations of East and West. Although representatives from twenty countries attended the Helsinki meeting, all Western delegates refused to join the organisation when it became apparent that it would be entirely under Communist leadership.

The only contacts the O.I.R.T. subsequently had with radio organisations outside the Communist bloc were with Finland, Iraq and Egypt – until the Bamako conference in 1961. Since then Mali, Guinea and Morocco have formally joined the organisation.

It has undertaken to help with the construction of the 'Voice of Africa' radio station decided upon at the Bamako conference, and will also train Africans in radio and television work, with special emphasis on the presentation of news to radio and television audiences.

The Women's International

The Women's International Democratic Federation (W.I.D.F.) plays an important role in Africa. Unlike some other front organisations, it has never pretended not to be a Communist movement. It was formed in 1945 on the initiative of a French Communist women's organisation, the *Union des Femmes Françaises*, and its President, Eugénie Cotton, is a Lenin Peace Prize winner and a Vice-President of the Communist-sponsored World Peace Council.

From the outset the W.I.D.F. has been active in underdeveloped countries and one of its subsidiary organisations, the International Committee for the Defence of the Rights of Children, has as a specific aim the easing of the plight of children exposed to 'imperialist aggression' and who are 'oppressed by colonialism.'

The emergence of African women as a political factor, a very recent phenomenon, has in fact opened a vast field of activity for the W.I.D.F., particularly as African women are largely ignored by Western political agencies. Any international organisation which professes to take African women seriously or which attempts to give them a share in political life is assured of a warm response, and the W.I.D.F. was certainly first in the field.

The propaganda department of the W.I.D.F. has since 1957 bombarded African women with literature (well illustrated for those who cannot read) dealing with such subjects as women's suffrage, polygamy, and social conditions, always stressing the oppression and suppression practised by the colonial Powers in contrast with the brilliant future offered under Communist bloc leadership.

Selected African women have been appointed officers of the W.I.D.F., the most notable example being Mrs Funmilayo Ransome-Kuti, President of the Federation of Nigerian Women's Unions and leader of the women's wing of the National Council of Nigeria and the Cameroons, who has been made a Vice-President.

Among African women's organisations now officially affiliated to the W.I.D.F. are the Union of Democratic Women of Cameroun (outlawed but still active as an underground organisation, closely associated with the terrorist uprising), the Union of Mali Women, the Union of Senegalese Women, the Ghana Council of Women and numerous others.

A number of regional conferences in Africa have been held under its auspices. Typical of these was the West African Women's Conference held in Conakry in July 1961. Resolutions adopted called for a struggle against imperialist military bases in Africa, and an intensification of the struggle for independence and liberty. Messages in support of these resolutions were sent by the Soviet Council of Women, the National Federation of Women of China, and the Vietnam Women's Union.

Since early 1961 the W.I.D.F. has organised regular visits by African women to Iron Curtain countries as guests of the affiliated women's organisations there. The African women are invariably given red carpet treatment and are entertained by the Head of State or Prime Minister.

Many of them are bewildered by such treatment, but enough are impressed and flattered to return to Africa to spread useful propaganda. The more intelligent and better educated are given courses of instruction lasting up to two months to prepare them for active organisation work in their home countries.

It is difficult to deny that African women have been sadly neglected by the colonial Powers and that little has been done for them under colonial rule (although much of this neglect has been due to male African insistence), but it cannot be argued that the W.I.D.F. contributes much to their emancipation by turning them into political tools to serve Communism. Significantly, in areas such as the Rhodesias, where a marked effort has been made to improve the lot of African women, the W.I.D.F. has made little progress.

In Kenya where strict tribal laws previously frustrated nearly all efforts to help women, the W.I.D.F. is rapidly gaining ground in the suddenly changed political atmosphere which has coincided with the recent Western abrogation of its duties towards undeveloped Africa. This trend seems likely to continue.

Work Among Africa's Youth

Important as the work of the W.I.D.F. is, it does not compare in effectiveness with that of the two international Communist youth organisations, the World Federation of Democratic Youth and the International Union of Students. Their activities must be considered separate from the actual education provided by the Soviet bloc because they are outright political movements operating under the direction of the Soviet Communist Youth League, *Komsomol*.

The World Federation of Democratic Youth (W.F.D.Y.) was founded in 1945 at a World Youth Conference in London but sponsored by the Communist-dominated World Youth Council. At first it was a non-political organisation but control soon passed into Communist hands. By 1949 all non-Communist youth movements had broken away to form their own international organisations, notably the World Assembly of Youth and the Union of Socialist Youth.

The W.F.D.Y. has its headquarters in Budapest. Its secretary-general is a French Communist, Christian Echard, who is a member of the executive of the Union of French Communist Youth Organisations. His two principal deputies are V. Shevchenko, of *Komsomol*, and Bara Lo of Senegal.

The President, Piero Pieralli, is a member of the Italian Communist Party; the Vice-Presidents include Sergei Pavlov, first secretary of *Komsomol*, and Mahmoud Gaafar, a Sudanese who went into exile when the Sudanese Communist Party was banned in 1958. He lives in Prague. Not one of the W.F.D.Y. leaders is under thirty years of age.

Although there is today not a single non-Communist youth movement in Europe (or America) affiliated to the W.F.D.Y., more than fifty African youth organisations are known to be, and most of them have become affiliated within the last two years. This suggests a sad lapse on the part of Western European and American youth organisations which have allowed their interest in Africa and friendship towards young Africans to be almost nullified by the Communist organisation.

A real spurt in the W.F.D.Y. wooing of African youth came in March 1961 when its Executive Committee astutely met in Conakry. Its widely publicised agenda consisted of two items: (1) The strengthening of the solidarity of youth the world over and the fight of African youth for the reconquest and consolidation of independence and unity in Africa; and (2) the role of W.F.D.Y. in the new world situation.

The same month the All-African Peoples' Conference, meeting in Accra, passed a resolution calling for the setting up of an all-African youth organisation. The W.F.D.Y. reacted immediately by convening what it called a seminar to discuss steps to be taken to give effect to the A.A.P.C.'s resolution. This was held in Casablanca in June.

Mahmoud Gafaar (the W.F.D.Y.'s Sudanese Vice-President mentioned above) could, as an indigenous African, take a prominent part in the seminar and he spoke with vigour about

the W.F.D.Y.'s support not only for the Algerian and Ango-
lese people but for all other Africans 'struggling against
colonialism and neo-colonialism.' He also condemned the
'aggressive face of U.S. imperialism and its Nato allies.'

Youth movements from twenty-two African countries sent
delegations to the seminar, but it ended without the promised
all-African youth organisation having been created. It did,
however, serve as a useful forerunner to the World Youth
Forum which was held in Moscow at the end of July and
early August 1961. Of the fifty delegations from thirty
African countries which were said to have attended the
Moscow rally (many with all expenses paid by the W.F.D.Y.),
a number are certain to have been recruited from among those
who attended the Casablanca seminar.

The Moscow Rally

As with previous Communist-sponsored world youth rallies,
every effort was made to give the Moscow gathering the
appearance of a truly international meeting. Delegations from
altogether 115 countries were invited, but it remained a Communist rally organised jointly by the W.F.D.Y. and the
International Union of Students.

For the opening session Khrushchev sent a message in which
he said: 'The young generation is making a great contribution
to the selfless struggle of the peoples against the most disgraceful form of man's oppression – colonialism.' This set the tone
and disclosed that the rally would focus its attention on
Africa.

A report was accordingly delivered on 'Youth and the
Struggle against Colonialism and for Independence.' In a
fighting speech, Sergei Pavlov, first secretary of *Komsomol*,
bitterly denounced the World Assembly of Youth and the
International Union of Socialist Youth, both of which had
refused to have anything to do with the Moscow rally.

A Ghanaian delegate, S. William, proclaimed that the time had come to draw up a charter defining the rights of youth, and a joint declaration from the delegations from the Portuguese African territories called on all present to demonstrate 'solidarity in the struggle against Portuguese colonialism and the Fascist tyranny of Salazar.'

At the end of the rally the African participants were taken on a free ten-day tour of the Soviet Union and lavishly entertained.

Although it was announced that fifty delegations from thirty African countries attended, few details were given. From various sources it was, however, learnt that Louis Akunda, who was Gizenga's 'Minister for Youth and Sport,' had come from the Congo with a delegation, that another delegation represented the outlawed Camerounian Democratic Youth, and that others included at least five delegates from Mali, three from Senegal, one from Kenya, nine from Ghana, nine from Guinea and one from Ethiopia.

Cementing Relations

Whatever else the Moscow gathering may have achieved, it undoubtedly made a deep impression on the African delegates, and the W.F.D.Y. has been quick to follow up the advantage gained. Under its direction Iron Curtain youth organisations are now working ceaselessly to increase the contacts and liaison they have been able to establish.

The rapidly developing relations with Ghana will serve as an example. At least three separate training courses on the technique of youth organisation have been held for Ghanaian Young Pioneers (a branch of the youth organisation of Nkrumah's Convention People's Party) at youth training camps in Moscow. One course, lasting seven months, was attended by ten officials from the Ghanaian Young Pioneers; another, lasting ten months, was attended by twenty-seven

Young Pioneers; and a third, of unspecified duration, was attended by a further ten Young Pioneers.

In Prague twenty Ghanaian day nursery officials attended a course on day nursery organisation (on scholarships made available by the W.F.D.Y.). In East Germany the Federation of German Youth has started special two-month courses in youth organisation for Ghanaian Young Pioneers and at Leipzig three-month courses for officials of the Ghana Central Organisation for Sport have been instituted.

An agreement has been concluded between Ghana's Young Pioneer movement and the Federation of East German Youth for 'permanent consultation' between the two organisations and for continued close co-operation. Jacob Stephens, director of the Kwame Nkrumah School for Youth Functionaries in Accra, has recently called for an 'intensification of the existing friendly relations with East Germany.'

It seems that separate East European countries have been allotted the responsibility of building up close relations with the youth movements of individual African countries. Thus, while East Germany is paying particular attention to Ghana, Czechoslovakia is concentrating on Guinea and Mali, Hungary on Somalia, and so on, but there is no water-tight demarcation. 'International' children's camps in East Germany, Poland and Czechoslovakia have been entertaining groups of Ghanaian Young Pioneers in equal numbers.

The Communist youth association of France,. *Union des Jeunesses Communistes de France*, one of whose leaders is the secretary-general of the W.F.D.Y., plays a singularly important part in fostering 'democratic' youth organisations in the former French territories, and recently East Germany has put out feelers to youth organisations in the erstwhile German territories – Cameroun, Togo, Tanganyika and Ruanda-Urundi.

Moscow therefore can review with satisfaction the work

done in Africa by the W.F.D.Y. during the past two years, particularly as there is no sign of its activities being checked. It has, however, yet to penetrate southern Africa.

Students' International

The International Union of Students (I.U.S.), which is also closely linked to *Komsomol*, was formed in Prague in 1946 and its headquarters has remained there. As in the case of the W.F.D.Y., it was originally presented to the world as a genuine international students' movement, and at first accepted as such.

By 1954, however, control had become so firmly vested in Communist hands that the students' unions of fourteen non-Communist countries had severed all links with it and had established their own international organisation, the Co-ordinating Secretariat of National Unions of Students.

The I.U.S. President is Jiri Pelikan, secretary of the Prague district of the Czechoslovakian Communist Party. The Vice-President with immediate responsibility for its activities in Africa is a Sudanese, Ettaveb Abu Gidary, who lives in exile in Prague. Another Vice-President is Zoya Tumanova, a former member of the Central Committee of the Communist Party of the Soviet Union.

The I.U.S. headquarters has a special department to direct the 'student fight against colonialism.' The head of it is a Persian in his late thirties, Houchang Saadati, who also uses the names Saadati Babak, Sadeq Babak, Sadek Jaafar, Kosravi and Amirkosravi.

With the failure of the I.U.S. to penetrate or influence the student world of Western Europe or North America, its activities are now directed mainly towards South America and Africa, and its greatest success so far has been in West Africa.

Affiliated to it are the Federation of Students from Black Africa Studying in France, the West African Students' Union in Britain, the General Union of West African Students (which is in France), and the General Union of Students in Portuguese Colonies. So are the organisations of African students in the various Communist bloc countries, such as the unions of African students in East Germany, Poland, Russia and China. The I.U.S. leaders have on a number of occasions admitted in public speeches that since students play a leading role in the 'liberation movement' of colonial people, the I.U.S. 'gives them all possible help.' It also makes scholarships available to African students, but with whose money is not clear.

In 1961 a number of 'Africa Day' rallies and 'International Youth Solidarity Days Against Colonialism' were organised by the I.U.S. in Moscow, Bucharest, Prague, Leipzig and other centres, all attended by delegations of African students. A major success was the Moscow rally from which Moscow Radio's African services were able to broadcast speeches by students from Kenya, Sierra Leone, Guinea, Mali, the Congo, Uganda, Ghana and Togo.

Another notable success was an 'international seminar' held in Bucharest. This, it was claimed, was attended by delegates from fifty countries including all West African States and Somalia, Kenya and Uganda. A communiqué issued afterwards said that it had been agreed that colonialism and imperialism must be denounced with greater vigour, and also that West German militarism was a threat to Africa.

Another student seminar, organised by the I.U.S. at Hanoi, Vietnam, and attended by delegates from Algeria, Cameroun, Ghana, Guinea, Portuguese Guinea, Morocco, Nigeria, Senegal and Togo, attacked the 'colonialist system of education.' There are many other examples, but these will suffice.

The I.U.S. does not yet operate on the same large scale as the W.F.D.Y., but its activities and influence in Africa are on the increase.

*   *   *

These then, are the Communist front organisations most active in Africa, which have already made a deep impact. Others, such as the World Federation of Teachers' Unions, the International Association of Democratic Lawyers, the International Federation of Resistance Fighters and the World Federation of Doctors, are also making strenuous efforts to win affiliations in Africa, but so far their impact has been less. It may not remain so, and their progress needs watching.

7

INDOCTRINATING YOUTH

It is not necessary to have an intimate knowledge of Africa to realise that lack of education is in the long run the continent's most vulnerable point. A century of neglect by the colonial Powers has left illiterate more than 90 per cent of all Africans south of the Sahara and many of the remaining 10 per cent would, by European standards, be regarded as near-illiterate.

The West is now doing its utmost to improve the position, but only an emergency operation is possible. Education takes time; it cannot be speeded up.

Whatever course the struggle between East and West takes, the provision of education for Africa's masses is a sound political investment; long before there was a recognisable Soviet policy towards Africa, Russia was welcoming young Africans to her schools and universities. In the nineteen thirties and forties they were mostly genuine students, many of whom had already been educated in Britain, France or Italy.

In the early nineteen fifties the first serious Communist efforts were made to recruit students direct from Africa, to get young Africans who had not already been contaminated by study in a West European country. But education for Africans presents problems and Russia's lack of previous contact had left her singularly ill-equipped to penetrate the mind of the unsophisticated African. Although the number of Africans receiving their education in the Soviet Union increased year by year, it remained a hit-and-miss operation, leaving Russia with little to show for her efforts.

East Germany Takes the Lead

In 1954 the subject was raised at a meeting of satellite leaders in Moscow. The East German delegates pointed out that among the countries within the Soviet bloc Germany had the soundest knowledge of Africa and the Africans.

Those in Moscow concerned with the problem had apparently forgotten that until the First World War Germany had been an important colonial Power with an impressive African empire in parts of West, Central and East Africa. Although the Treaty of Versailles had deprived Germany of her African possessions, large German communities had remained there for many years.

The outcome was that the East German Government was asked to study the problem and to make specific recommendations.

The East German study of the subject began with 500 specially selected young Africans from Ghana, Guinea, Nigeria, Somalia (then still two separate territories), Togo, the then French Cameroons, Zanzibar, the Ivory Coast, Angola, Morocco and Algeria. The Germans were certainly thorough in picking their cross-section.

A special department was created in the East German Ministry for Higher Education to give these 500 Africans special attention, and a corps of reliable German students was recruited to supervise their day-to-day activities. The Africans were no doubt unaware that they were guinea pigs in an experiment which was to result in an educational offensive in Africa.

The reports which the East German Ministry for Higher Education submitted to Moscow were apparently so satisfactory and encouraging that in 1958 the Soviet Union asked for a special study to be made of the role education can play in the 'national liberation struggle.' This was discussed at a special conference convened at the Humboldt University in East Berlin in November that year.

As part of this further study three new training establishments for young Africans were founded. They are the 'Solidarity School' at the Wilhelm Pieck Youth College at Bautzen, the 'Ideological College' at Bogensee and the 'School for International Friendship' at Bernau. In addition, an African Institute was set up at the Karl Marx University in Leipzig, and Professor Georg Mayer of this university was asked to prepare recommendations on how to link African education with the 'anti-imperialist struggle waged by the under-developed countries.'

Since then the Karl Marx University has instituted study groups, with Africans participating, to examine the menace of 'neo-colonialism.' These study groups have come to the conclusion that 'the best development aid the imperialist can give the national States is to leave Africa as quickly as possible.'

The Lumumba University

Russia was for once willing to learn from one of her satellites and the present Soviet educational policy for Africa is very much of East German origin. One recommendation was that separate institutions should be established especially to meet the needs of young Africans.

One result was the creation of the People's Friendship University outside Moscow, which has since been renamed the Patrice Lumumba Friendship University in memory of the late Congolese leader.

The first announcement that this university was to be established was made by Khrushchev in February 1960, while on a visit to Indonesia. Addressing the students of Jogjakarta University, he said: 'The Soviet Union is giving economic aid to countries which ask for it. But the people's needs are not limited to economic aid. They are in dire need of more education and of *creating national cadres which will understand correctly the interests of their country . . . and will work for the strengthening of the economic and political independence of their motherland.'* (The italics are, of course, mine.)

To establish a university exclusively for Africans would have been too blatant, and according to the original announcement students from all under-developed countries were to be accepted. It was left to the Rector, Professor S. V. Rumyantsev, a former Deputy Minister for Higher Education, to make the subsequent announcement that, in the selection of students, priority would be given to Africans.

The Friendship University opened on October 1 1960. It will by 1963 have accommodation for up to 4,000 students. By then it will have its own buildings, but provisionally it has taken over a former military academy, and a former military barracks is at present used as a hostel. Because of lack of accommodation, only 600 students had been enrolled by the opening date, and in 1961 there were only 700. At the end of 1961 it was announced that the full number of 4,000 will be admitted in 1963.

The university offers four-year courses in engineering, agriculture, economics, teaching and other subjects. It also accepts young Africans without the qualifications necessary to enter a university. For them there is a preparatory faculty where they can study Russian and general subjects for up to three years before entering the university proper. The age limit for students is thirty-five.

It was originally announced that no Russian students would attend the Friendship University. This decision was subsequently changed, the explanation given being that it had been decided that a 'small contingent' of Russians would help foreign students to learn Russian and would give them more contact with Soviet life. A less charitable explanation is that selected Soviet students are useful to supervise the activities of foreign students, as had been the case with the German experiment.

So great is the thirst for education in every part of Africa that there is no reason to disbelieve a statement by the university's Pro-Rector, Professor P. V. Yerzin, that 30,000 applications for admittance were received before the opening date. It should be added that Moscow Radio in its African service and all other Communist propaganda media had given wide publicity to the creation of the Friendship University. Applications need not pass through any recognised educational or official channel. They can be made direct to the university or to any Soviet diplomatic representative.

It is relevant to quote the opinion of one student who has attended the Friendship University. He is a Sudanese, Mustapha Abul Majid, who said after he had left Moscow: 'The Friendship University stipulates that whoever wishes to join it should submit a sort of autobiography, to enable the board of directors to confirm that the applicant has Communist inclinations and that he is willing to be converted to Communism.'

If accepted, all the applicant's expenses are paid, including his travel from home, and apart from having all his needs supplied he is given a cash allowance. This method of direct recruitment has caused misgivings in several countries. Chief Okotie-Eboh, Nigeria's Finance Minister, has commented on the peculiar fact that almost none of the Nigerian students in Moscow possesses a passport, and the Nepalese Minister for Education has stated bluntly that he will not allow any Nepalese student to attend this peculiar university.

Peculiar is not too strong a word to use. Professor Rumyantsev has given the purpose of the Friendship University as being to train a 'national intelligentsia' for under-developed countries which will be able to bring 'all-round social progress.' Translated into everyday language this means to set up a Communist regime. He added that in training the national intelligentsia, Russia is able to draw on her experience in building up cadres in the republics of Soviet Central Asia.

A Nigerian student, Anthony G. Okotcha, maintains that he was given straightforward training as a revolutionary agent. Plans with which he was entrusted called for assassination, terrorist acts, arson and the use of Communist-indoctrinated witch-doctors.

Czechoslovakia Joins the Experiment

The Friendship University experiment seems to have been a success from the Soviet point of view, because one year after it opened the Czechoslovak Government announced that it was founding a similar university in Prague, to be called the University of November 17th (to commemorate the day in 1939 when Hitler closed the Czech high schools and executed a number of Czech students).

This Czech establishment opened at the end of 1961, in temporary buildings while three permanent buildings are being constructed. Also designed specifically for students from under-developed countries with preference for African students, it specialises in courses intended, according to the Czech Ministry for Education, 'to cover the needs of the countries concerned.'

In due course, the Ministry has announced, this university will control the studies in Czechoslovakia of all students from under-developed countries. At the opening ceremony the Czech Minister for Education and Culture, Dr F. Kahuda, said: 'The main reason for erecting the new university is to support the justified fight of the countries of Asia, Africa and Latin America for political, economic and cultural independence.'

Also present at the opening was the chief of the Russian Centre for Foreign Students at Soviet Universities, K. N.

Kulikov, who works under the direction of the Soviet Government Department for Relations with Foreign Communist Parties. General B. Lastovicka, who was at one time in charge of political education in the Czechoslovakian armed forces and at another time Czech Ambassador in Moscow, was there too.

Other Establishments

Apart from these experiments with special universities, the normal educational establishments of Russia and the satellite countries are increasing their intake of African students. According to the present Soviet Deputy Minister for Higher Education, Mikhail Prokofyev, there were at the beginning of 1961 more than 12,000 students from under-developed countries in Soviet universities and high schools. Most of these were from Africa.

As well as the better-known universities like Moscow, Leningrad and Kiev, they are to be found in such remote places as the Georgian Polytechnic Institute at Tiflis, the Central Asian State University at Tashkent, Uzbekistan, and several others. In 1961 it was announced that students from Northern and Southern Rhodesia, Kenya, the Sudan, Nigeria, Sierra Leone, Zanzibar, Somalia, Togo, Cameroun, Guinea and Ghana had been awarded scholarships by the Soviet Afro-Asian Solidarity Committee to study at Soviet Asian high schools and universities.

Czechoslovakia is similarly increasing her facilities for African students. According to Radio Prague there are well over 3,000 Africans at Czech high schools and universities. Like Russia, she accepts young Africans who are in no way ready for any form of higher education. A special school for them has been established at Teplice, in Northern Bohemia, where 350 semi-illiterates can be accommodated at a time.

Poland, Rumania, Hungary and Bulgaria have also joined the drive to educate Africans. Early in 1961 the Warsaw weekly, *Polityka,* criticised what it called Polish apathy in this field. 'The strengthening and the economic and cultural development of African countries,' it wrote, 'are of the same importance as the strengthening and development of the freedom zone; consequently they are of great importance to us.'

Shortly afterwards *Polityka* opened a 'Patrice Lumumba Scholarship Fund' to enable more Africans to study at Polish high schools. Within a fortnight more than one million zlotys had been contributed. The Polish Academy of Sciences has, incidentally, given two annual scholarships to enable African students to study 'atomic science' under the auspices of the Polish State Council for the Peaceful Use of Atomic Energy.

Outside the field of normal schooling the Communist bloc countries have started the training of administrative personnel. The Soviet Union, for instance, has inaugurated courses in banking for what she calls finance workers from Ghana, and both the Moscow Co-operative Institute and the Soviet Industrial Technical Co-operative School have agreed to accept African co-operative officials for training. Special courses in national economic planning have recently been added to the range of subjects taught at the Friendship University.

Czechoslovakia, too, has started special ten-week courses for Africans at the Central Co-operative School near Prague, and East Germany has invited African co-operative societies to send officials for training by the East German Association of Co-operative Societies. By the end of 1961 Africans from Ghana, Uganda, Kenya and Togo were listed as attending these schools.

It is possible to give an almost endless list of similar examples.

Schooling in Africa

Another important step in the past year is the attempt to provide schooling in Africa itself and in this way to penetrate the existing educational systems in African countries. Although this effort is still in its early stages, good progress is being made.

The aim of this policy was outlined at a meeting of the Communist-sponsored World Federation of Teachers' Unions held in Prague at the end of June 1961. It emphasised the importance of 'establishing democratic and national school systems in the new countries in Africa . . . so as to ensure their independence,' and of 'fighting cultural aggression where reactionary ideology and pedagogy are being forced on underdeveloped countries under the guise of cultural aid, especially as practised by the U.S.A.'

Notable success has so far been achieved in Guinea, Mali and Somalia, and the Ghanaian educational system has also been penetrated.

Russia has presented Guinea with a complete polytechnical institute. Described as the first higher educational establishment in Guinea, it is now under construction and is due to open at the beginning of 1963 with 1,600 students.

According to Moscow Radio it will become the largest establishment for teaching technology in Africa and will have a library of 170,000 books, a stadium to seat 25,000 and a conference hall to seat 700. Apart from this the Soviet Deputy Minister for Culture, Aleksander Kutznetsov, has been able to announce his complete satisfaction with the number of Soviet teachers now teaching in schools in Guinea, although no figures have been given.

In Ghana, Nkrumah's announced plan to recruit lecturers in Russia and Poland led to angry demonstrations by students. This did not deter him and the first significant appointment followed in September 1961 when Dr Jan Drewnowski of the

Polish Central School of Planning and Statistics was appointed Professor of Economics at Accra University. This was followed by an announcement that the Soviet Academy of Sciences was to train Ghanaian science teachers.

Mali has gone further. In September 1961 it was announced in Prague that the Czechoslovak Ministry of Education was to undertake, at the request of the Mali Ministry of Education, the task of completely reorganising the Mali educational system.

Czechoslovakia is also building a technical college in Somalia and will provide all the equipment and teachers, who will stay for eight years while they train Somali teachers to take over.

Elsewhere in the Horn of Africa, a cultural agreement concluded between Russia and Ethiopia in April 1961 provides for Soviet teachers to staff the science faculty at Addis Ababa University College. Russia has furthermore undertaken to build and staff, as a gift, a technical school for 1,000 pupils. It will open in October 1963.

In East Germany it has been announced that the Dresden Technical College library has established close relations with twenty-six unspecified educational establishments in the new States in Africa and has arranged to equip their libraries for them.

'No Charity'

It is, of course, true that the countries of the West are educating a considerably larger number of Africans (in Britain alone there are about 40,000 overseas students). The kind of education provided by Western universities and high schools cannot, however, be compared with that given in Communist countries.

Communist education is specifically designed to turn out African Communists or at least Soviet agents who are to play a part in the struggle for Africa. In the West, young Africans receive a normal education, which sometimes turns them into Communists and sometimes does not. In the Communist world the education they receive is far from normal and far from innocent.

The Africans who are accepted by the Communist countries are carefully selected – but not for their aptitude for learning. The almost illiterate are just as acceptable for so-called higher education as Africans who have already qualified in the West. They are selected on the basis of their suitability for conversion into Soviet fifth columnists, and seldom for any other reason.

The final comment I shall leave to the Czechoslovakian newspaper, *Zemedelske Noviny*, which has stated candidly: 'We don't invite students from colonial countries out of charity.'

8

THE PROPAGANDA OFFENSIVE

Are the Russians better propagandists than their counterparts in the West? There is no clear answer to the question. If the yardstick is merely whether Communist propaganda makes a deeper impact on Africans than Western propaganda, then the answer must be yes. But is that a fair yardstick?

Communist and Western propaganda pursue two different aims.

The B.B.C. or Voice of America may at times deserve criticism, but their broadcasts to African countries are at least influenced by one consideration: they strive to convey the truth. Comment may sometimes be biased, but the underlying objective is to make facts known, to tell the Africans the truth about matters affecting Africa, even if the truth is not always favourable to Western interests.

To use a Communist phrase, Western propaganda to Africa often indulges in self-criticism. British propaganda is, furthermore, often critical of America, and the other way round. British and American propaganda is often also mutually contradictory and as a result confuses many Africans.

And then, of course, truth is usually less dramatic than political fiction: during political discussions among Africans it is much more satisfying to discuss Europeans as devils than as philanthropists or well-meaning idealists. Moscow Radio's blood and thunder is much more interesting and stimulating.

Soviet propaganda can give the Africans what they like to hear, particularly as Moscow has no responsibility for carrying out a day-to-day policy closely linked with the welfare of the people. Moscow Radio can afford to be utterly irresponsible, and if its broadcasts actually cause violence, it is often so much the better pleased.

In the circumstances it is not surprising that Russian propaganda makes a deeper impact.

Russian propagandists are perhaps more experienced in influencing backward peoples who have little or no access to other sources of news. Forty or more years of experience in Soviet Asia have taught many lessons; so has propaganda work among Bulgarian or Rumanian peasants. This is not off-set by the fact that many Britons have had years of intimate experience of Africa. Colonial Office officials and European settlers or businessmen are not necessarily good propagandists.

And unfortunately not many Americans know Africa.

Reference has already been made to the work of the several thousand Communist bloc experts who are in Africa, all working to a definite plan. Whatever else these people may be expert in, they are all carefully trained propagandists, whether they are ostensibly technicians, economic planners or military instructors. Backing them up all the time, providing the right background for their efforts, is Moscow Radio, transmitting from several stations and supported by satellite radio campaigns.

Moscow Radio Joins the Offensive

For at least a decade there has been talk of Communist propaganda in Africa, but there is no evidence that Moscow paid much attention to the matter until 1958.

Soviet broadcasts to Africa began in April that year. The beginning was small and experimental, confined to fifteen minutes daily in English and French. The broadcasts came through loud and clear and the response appears to have satisfied the Russians who, in November of the same year, increased the time to a total of five and a half hours a week. This was, however, still a negligible effort.

The first significant increase came one year later, in November 1959, when the broadcasts were stepped up to 31½ hours a week (two hours daily in English and two and a half hours in French). From now on there were also occasional broadcasts in Swahili, beamed to East Africa. Now, too, the programmes became decidedly political, whereas previously they were merely interesting and entertaining, designed to build up a listening audience.

One particularly important programme was presented regularly by no less a person than Professor Potekhin himself on behalf of the Soviet-African Friendship Association of which he is chairman. Strongly anti-West, the main emphasis of this programme was from the outset on the evils of colonialism. It was clearly designed to flatter African nationalist aspirations and to hold the Soviet Union up as Africa's true friend.

Another programme introduced at this time was called 'As Africans see the U.S.S.R.' and consisted of talks on Russia by African students at Soviet universities or Africans visiting Russia. It was in this programme that the first broadcast in Swahili was made – by a Uganda student then attending Moscow University.

Special programmes for African women and young people followed, and a 'pen friends club' was started. A quiz programme offered 'valuable' prizes for answers to questions about Russia, but to make it easy or to stimulate interest, preliminary talks were given to provide the answers.

In October 1959 Prague Radio began to supplement these broadcasts with special transmissions in French to Africa south of the Sahara.

In February 1960 regular broadcasts began in Swahili, and

during the year East Germany, Poland, Rumania and Bulgaria also introduced regular transmissions to Africa, Czechoslovakia and Rumania, adding Portuguese transmissions to their repertoire.

The Radio Offensive is Stepped Up

Nineteen sixty-one brought a major advance in the radio onslaught on Africa. In February, Moscow Radio began several new programmes. One was a feature series called 'The Voice of the Soviet Afro-Asian Solidarity Committee,' and listeners were invited to get in touch with the Committee by writing to 10, Kropotkin Street, Moscow. Another new programme provided Russian lessons, and it was announced that the text of the broadcasts, textbooks and any other literature would be sent free to any African asking for it.

In April broadcasts in Amharic were started by Moscow Radio, and in August broadcasts in Portuguese. By the end of August Moscow Radio and the satellite radios were beaming programmes to Africa for 114 hours a week. The allocation was then as follows:

Russia: English, 19¼ hours; French, 19¼ hours; Swahili, 7 hours; Amharic, 3½ hours; and Portuguese, 7 hours. Total: 56 hours.
East Germany: English, 5¼ hours; French, 5¼ hours; Total: 10½ hours.
Czechoslovakia: English, 7 hours; French, 7 hours; and Portuguese, 3 hours. Total: 17 hours.
Poland: English, 10½ hours; French, 10½ hours. Total: 21 hours.
Bulgaria: French, 6 hours.
Rumania: Portuguese, 3½ hours.

Two months later, in October 1961, Moscow Radio introduced transmissions in Italian beamed to Somalia for the benefit of the large part of that country which had been under Italian rule until independence in July 1960, and therefore subject to Italian cultural influence. Potekhin gave the first broadcast, in which he said that the new service would 'contribute to the further consolidation of friendship and understanding between the Soviet and Somali people.'

By the end of 1961 Moscow Radio had increased its output to Africa by a further one-third, adding 17½ hours to its previous total of fifty-six hours a week, to make a total of 131½ hours a week from Moscow and the European satellites. This figure, as in the case of the previous total of 114 hours, does not include the considerable time devoted to the Arabic service.

I have not included the Arabic service, which is older than the various African services, as it does not form part of the Communist effort to penetrate Africa south of the Sahara. Admittedly, however, the Arab-speaking population of both Somalia and Zanzibar as well as the Arab minorities in Kenya and Tanganyika can and do listen to these transmissions. But the Arabic service does not deal specifically with the affairs of black Africa.

Moscow Radio's weekly programmes to Africa were by the end of the year: Amharic, 7 hours; Swahili, 14 hours; English, 21 hours; French, 21 hours; Italian, 3½ hours, Portuguese, 7 hours.

Focus on East Africa

The significant increases were in transmissions to East Africa and Somalia. While the English and French broadcasts were increased by about fifteen minutes a day, the Swahili service was doubled – from seven to fourteen hours a week – at precisely the time when the Swahili-speaking countries (Uganda, Kenya, Tanganyika and Zanzibar) were entering a decisive political phase.

Moscow has also revised its estimate of the number of people who use Swahili as a *lingua franca*. Previously, according to the Large Soviet Encyclopaedia, Swahili was thought to be spoken by 10 to 15 million Africans. The revised estimate, given in the *Sovietskaya Ethnografiya*, places the figure at 20 to 30 million. It is, of course, true that Swahili is understood by many Africans as far away as the Congo, Mozambique, Nyasaland and Northern Rhodesia.

When Moscow Radio began an Italian service to Somalia, it almost simultaneously increased the broadcast time in Amharic, for Ethiopia. This is in line with Soviet policy of doing everything possible not to give offence to Ethiopia while actively wooing Somalia. It is a tight-rope which it requires considerable skill to walk, and it is still too soon to say whether Russia will succeed. There are few things Ethiopia is so sensitive about as friendship between any outside Power and Somalia.

Somalia is, however, a cornerstone in the present Soviet approach to Africa, and the gamble therefore appears to be thought justifiable. But it remains at best a calculated risk.

Peking Radio

Although the Chinese radio offensive in Africa is not the subject of this chapter, a comparison with Russian activities may be of interest. Peking Radio turned its attention to Africa a full two years before Moscow Radio. In late 1956 China introduced a daily programme of one hour, beamed to Africa in English morse at dictation speed. Its effectiveness was doubtful as the number of Africans who can read morse is negligible.

In November 1958 Peking Radio introduced a daily programme in Cantonese for the Chinese minorities in south and south-east Africa and Madagascar. These programmes were on the whole innocuous and were probably mainly experimental to determine the technical feasibility of broadcasting effectively from China to Africa. China did not want to begin a proper African service until all the technical problems had been smoothed out.

The broadcasts in Cantonese enabled the Chinese engineers to determine the best wavelengths and strength. Not being a signatory to the international agreement regulating these matters, China could do as she pleased, regardless of whether she was blasting other radio broadcasts off the air or making them incomprehensible. By September 1959 all technical difficulties had been overcome, and Peking Radio introduced a daily two-hour programme beamed to Africa in English.

The service expanded rapidly and within two years it temporarily exceeded the total time Moscow Radio was devoting to Africa. In August 1961 Peking Radio's African service devoted 35 hours weekly to programmes in English, seven hours to Portuguese, seven hours to Cantonese, seven hours to Swahili; plus four hours to French programmes which were not directed solely at Africa, and an additional three hours to English which also did not have Africa as exclusive target. Peking Radio's Arabic service is not included in these figures.

From experience I can testify that no other radio programmes can be heard as clearly in all parts of Africa as those of Peking Radio. And they are excellent – entertaining, instructive and interesting, well worth any listener's attention.

At the end of 1961 it was reported that China was about to follow Russia's example in introducing regular Italian programmes for Somalia. It should be stressed that Peking Radio operates entirely independently of Moscow Radio. Unlike the European satellites, the Chinese programmes do not supplement those of Moscow. In fact they often clash with them, occasionally introduce an anti-Russian tone and generally leave no doubt that Peking Radio is the voice of an independent China deciding her own African policy.

Moscow's Message to Africa

The message contained in the Soviet radio propaganda campaign in Africa has been fairly consistent although there are many minor deviations to suit day-to-day political developments, to give practical guidance to African nationalist politicians and to acclaim or discredit particular leaders for the stand they have taken on any relevant issue of the moment.

The general theme was set by Potekhin in a talk given on October 30th, 1959. 'The Soviet people,' he said, 'show an enormous interest in the way of life of the African people . . . Africans have cause for pride before the other peoples of the world. In the remote past, before the European colonialists made their appearance, they had their own States. The names of some of these States, such as Ghana and Mali, are again appearing on the African map . . . The Soviet State has given, and will give, unselfish economic assistance to the African countries who have cast off colonialism and created their national States. In the U.S.S.R., all people fighting for peace and independence, especially the African people, have a loyal friend.'

On another occasion he said: 'The study of this (pre-colonial) period of history . . . has an important political significance. Casting off the yoke of colonialism, the people of Africa are now showing a great interest in their past. African scholars, assisted by the progressive scholars . . . are unmasking the lie of imperialistic propaganda, which maintains that the African people do not have a history of their own. The obligation of Marxist historians is to help in the restoration of historical truth.'

Telling attacks have been made on the 'fiction of *bourgeois* historians' that Europeans have played a civilising role in Africa. Special study has been devoted to such topics as Anglo-German competition in East Africa towards the end of the last century, French expansion in Africa, the struggle of the Zulus and the Xhosa against Anglo-Boer colonisation, the struggle of the Mashona and Matabele against the colonisation of Rhodesia, and others. It is claimed that this provides 'spiritual support for the peoples of Africa.'

Since the end of 1959 a constant theme has been the 'colonialist extermination' of millions of Africans. This, it is claimed, is proved by dwindling population figures in a number of territories. The Russians admit that there are no exact statistics to prove their claims, but it is, for instance, alleged that the population of the former French Equatorial Africa decreased from eight million in 1923 to two and a half million in 1932.

While it is true that no exact figures are available, the 1926 League of Nations *International Statistical Yearbook* estimated the population of French Equatorial Africa to have been slightly over three million in 1923; the United Nations *Demographic Yearbook* for 1958 gave the population of the same area as just on five million in 1957. That reveals a steady annual population increase of 1.8 per cent.

The theme is constant. On 'Africa Freedom Day' – April 15th, 1961 – the message was: 'The colonialists want Africans to live in the space age as they lived in the stone age . . . to vegetate in darkness and ignorance, and to be cheap slaves . . . unable to cope single-handed with the mighty wave of the national liberation struggle . . . The imperialists have created a holy alliance (*sic*) against the people of Africa.'

Similarly, in East Africa 'Britain intends to dismember Kenya . . . The idea of gradual constitutional development is merely a trick to preserve colonialism,' and on 'Uganda

Solidarity Day' – July 5th, 1961 – that country was 'still enduring the torments of imperialism.' In this case Britain was applying her 'savage policy of divide and rule' and inciting racialism to create a conflict among the population. As always, the struggling Africans would find their most powerful weapon to be 'unity with the Socialist countries.'

Moscow Radio has for some time been urging the people of Kenya in Swahili to reject any British proposals for constitutional reform. Jomo Kenyatta was for long Russia's hero in the exhortations to Kenya's Africans, and the people were constantly urged to demand his release while he was in semi-seclusion.

When complete freedom was eventually restored to Kenyatta, Moscow Radio claimed it to be 'the result of insistent demands and world opinion.' It also said in Swahili: 'The release of Kenyatta is a major victory for the national liberation movement in Kenya and a victory for the anti-colonialist forces of the world.'

Later, when Kenyatta's status as Kenya's national leader became more obscure, there were fewer and fewer references to him.

During the constitutional negotiations between the Kenya leaders and the Colonial Office, Moscow Radio did all it could to disrupt the proceedings by frantically urging non-co-operation with Britain. 'Though Africans have a majority in Kenya,' it proclaimed, 'all power is still with the colonialists ... The monopolists intend to continue the bankrupt policy of supporting the racists.' The African leader of the Kenya Democratic Union and others who did to some extent co-operate with the British authorities were described as having been hand-picked by the colonialists for their role as British stooges.

Early in 1962 Moscow Radio's verdict on Kenya was that British policy had placed it 'well on the way to becoming a new East African version of the Congo.' For once many Britons wholeheartedly agreed with Moscow.

Warnings Against Welensky

Since about the middle of 1961 Moscow Radio has paid close attention to developments in the Federation of Rhodesia and Nyasaland. Its broadcasts in English, beamed to southern Africa, can be heard clearly throughout the Federation. The Africans of all three territories of the Federation are repeatedly urged to support the more militant leaders, and the leaders themselves are given constant exhortations to resist British attempts to introduce any reforms which do not meet the most far-reaching demands.

Constantly warning the Africans against adopting a non-violent policy, Moscow Radio has told those in Northern Rhodesia outright that they must accept the fact that 'the struggle is assuming the character of a civil war' and must be ready for civil war if they want 'real independence and freedom.'

It has told the Africans all over the Federation that where 'intrigues have failed to secure the racist objective' of British business interest, which is 'to preserve white domination by depriving almost the whole African population of votes,' there was now a resort to 'blackmail and terror.' It added: 'The bestial morals of Rhodes persist.' Special warnings have been given against 'any solution devised by Welensky or London' because these would inevitably ignore the 'Africans' needs and rights.'

In Southern Rhodesia, according to Moscow Radio, the Government has resorted to 'Fascist action' to withhold the rights due to the Africans. Moscow's lack of first-hand knowledge of Rhodesia is, however, revealed when Southern Rhodesia's Africans are urged to follow the leadership of Dr Hastings Banda of Nyasaland, whose work represents a 'devastating defeat for the colonialists.' Better-informed propagandists would have known that the Africans of Southern Rhodesia, even the most extreme, have decided reservations about Banda as a nationalist leader.

America's Turn

The United States receives her full share of abuse in the broadcasts. For example, 'the United States under Kennedy is emerging more determined than ever to disrupt the African liberation struggle.' The main theme is that 'United States imperialism,' with its 'neo-colonialism,' is 'the greatest enemy of African independence,' and the United Nations is, as is to be expected, 'its tool.'

The Kennedy Administration has been 'dressing up as sympathisers of national independence . . . and using the so-called Peace Corps and other tactics to make Africans fight Africans.' The Kennedy Administration also 'emphasises the necessity for preparing a 'limited' and 'sub-limited' war, the aim of which is to send troops directly where necessary to suppress national democratic movements in Africa.'

Nato has become an instrument by which colonialism is to be extended in Africa, according to Moscow, and it follows therefore that all foreign troops and all foreign bases must be withdrawn from the continent. The Nato 'strongpoints' in Africa are designed 'to keep the African Continent in their (the imperialists') sphere of exploitation.' Therefore 'foreign military bases and foreign military troops on African territory are the sword of Damocles over the young African States.'

The colonial Powers (including the neo-colonialist United States) have in fact 'unmasked themselves as a united front against the people's national liberation movement.' Foreign military bases in Africa now stand revealed as a 'means of imperialistic interference in the internal affairs of young African States.'

It is possible to quote almost endlessly from Communist bloc broadcasts to Africa. But there would be no point in it. The few excerpts which have been given convey the tone and nature of the potent propaganda directed at unsophisticated people.

African Moderates Condemned

Faithful to the doctrine laid down by Potekhin, the earlier broadcasts from Moscow had praise for nearly all African leaders. In 1959 people such as Julius Nyerere of Tanganyika, Sir Abubakar Balewa of Nigeria, and Felix Houphouet-Boigny of the Ivory Coast were praised alongside Sekou Touré and Kwame Nkrumah. At that time Nyerere was said to be 'wresting independence for Tanganyika in a bitter struggle.'

But once independence has been attained, the leaders who remain moderate are discredited and subjected to outright denunciation. Felix Houphouet-Boigny, now President of the Ivory Coast, has been described by Moscow Radio as 'enemy number one of African unity.' President Ahidjo of Cameroun has become an 'acolyte' of the ex-colonial authorities, and both Nyerere and Sir Abubakar are now instruments of the imperialists. Every African leader who preaches moderation once independence for his country has been gained is condemned, and support is given to his militant opponents. The pattern does not vary.

Zuberi Mtemvu, leader of Tanganyika's small but extremist African National Congress, is now the Soviet hero there, and a number of Nigerian extremists are in the process of being built up by Communist propaganda as their country's only reliable nationalists. The propaganda is effective, and will in due course give much trouble to those African leaders who remain potentially friendly towards the West. It can bring disaster to any who actually wish their country to be aligned with the West.

Among the yardsticks used by Moscow propagandists to assess the real quality of an African nationalist leader once independence is achieved, is the speed with which he gets rid of the administrative machine, including European civil servants, which he inherits from the departing colonial Power.

This is a subject about which there is no argument among rational people – white or black. Colonial rule has provided the various African States with a framework which enables them to be administered according to well-tried, civilised methods. If that administrative machine collapses, almost everything else collapses with it – as has been proved by the Congo's tragic history since independence. But modern administration is something fairly new in Africa; there are not yet enough Africans available to carry on unaided the tradition they have inherited.

Enlightened African leaders retain the services of European officials to help them through a transition period – to keep the country concerned functioning smoothly while Africans are trained to take the Europeans' place. The Europeans who are retained on this basis become the servants of the independent African country concerned; they are not a rearguard of colonial rule. Moreover, the length of their stay will at all times be determined by the speed with which Africans can take over without the risk of an administrative breakdown.

Most responsible African leaders therefore go out of their way to induce key European personnel to remain and to enter their service. The African countries where the transition from European to African rule has been smoothest have, without exception, been the countries where this principle has been accepted.

Russians Are Not White

The prevention of chaos does not necessarily suit Moscow, especially if the new African rule proves to be moderate.

Furthermore, the retention of European officials often minimises Communist bloc influence. Moscow Radio therefore wages a continuous war against the whole concept.

No country is deemed free or independent until the last white man has been kicked out. If administrators are needed, Russians and East Europeans are available to help out; presumably they do not count as white. The late Patrice Lumumba is today still acclaimed for his show of nationalism in kicking out Belgian officials. The chaos which followed appears to be considered a tribute to his greatness.

Week after week Africans in all parts of Africa are told that the so-called achievements of the former colonial administrations are a pure myth, and that the retention of former officials is not only harmful to Africa's well-being but a positive danger to independence and an insult to African pride. This helps further to discredit moderate African rulers who wish to retain European help. The fact that even Ghana has hired her full share of Europeans and that Ethiopia, which has never been a colonial country, finds it necessary to rely on European advisers, is completely overlooked.

This propaganda is effective, as is most of Moscow's propaganda. The main reason why the effect is not more devastating is that few ordinary Africans, especially tribesmen, possess radio sets. But the politicians, especially the minor ones, come mostly from the towns and cities where radios are plentiful. It is among them that the impact of Soviet propaganda is most noticeable. And its effectiveness will increase.

9

MILITARY AID
(Legal and Otherwise)

It was fortunate for Britain, and for Kenya, that the Mau Mau uprising which began in 1953 took place before Russia had become an organised gun-runner into Africa. The Mau Mau terrorists, effective as they were, had to rely on crude, often home-made, fire-arms, on their spears and pangas and on what modern weapons they could steal.

It was not possible for Russia to give them effective material help. In 1953 the Sudan was still under British control. So was the then British Somaliland, and the former Italian Somaliland was still administered by Italy as a United Nations Trust territory. To the south, Tanganyika was ruled by Britain, as was Uganda in the north-west.

The only remaining overland route for a passage of arms was through Ethiopia – the almost impenetrable southern Ethiopia – which adjoins Kenya's Northern Frontier Province. But northern Kenya is largely inhabited by nomadic tribes, all hostile to the Kikuyu, who would not have tolerated help passing through their area to the Mau Mau.

If the Mau Mau had not been so isolated geographically the story of the uprising, gruesome as it was, might have been considerably more serious. A renewed outbreak of Mau Mau-ism after the departure of the British administration is certain to have a different outcome.

This time Soviet help will reach the terrorists. Since the last uprising a number of Kikuyu have received training in guerrilla and partisan warfare in Czechoslovakia and East Germany, and Communist bloc 'liaison officers' are ready for service in the field with the Mau Mau 'freedom fighters' or whatever they may call themselves next time.

It can therefore be taken for granted that Russia will not again be a mere sympathetic onlooker. Moscow Radio has already told Kenya's 'freedom fighters' in Swahili that they can in future rely on active support.

The form this will take has been seen in every part of Africa where there has been large-scale bloodshed in the last three years – Algeria, Cameroun, Angola, Portuguese Guinea, the Congo and even on the Ethiopian-Somali frontier. It should be noted that aid is not confined to anti-European activity. In Cameroun, for instance, it is in support of a bid to overthrow Ahidjo's moderate Government.

Communist military assistance in Africa is divided into two categories, one official and the other unofficial and clandestine.

The Example of Guinea

The official military links with emerging Africa (excluding the earlier arms deals with Egypt) began only in 1959, with Guinea. Today, however, close liaison exists with the entire Casablanca group of Powers – Ghana, Guinea, Mali, Egypt and Morocco – and there is strong support for this group's so-called 'African military high command,' set up for the purpose of providing assistance to militant extremist movements anywhere in Africa who wish to drive imperialists out.

The first foothold was won in March 1959 with the arrival in Conakry of a Czech military mission bringing a gift of arms. Although initially only 'visiting,' it was transformed into a resident mission. One of its first tasks was to reorganise Guinea's army and to provide a military training establishment. In 1960 the capacity of this establishment was increased to enable it to accept Africans from all parts of the African continent.

There is evidence that since then selected Africans from Kenya, Uganda, Rhodesia, Angola, Mozambique, the Congo, Portuguese Guinea and a number of former French territories have passed through it and returned to their home countries.

Control of Guinea's army has virtually passed to Czech 'liaison' officers, with the full approval of the Guinean Government. In addition, Guinea has provided the Communist bloc with its first military base in Africa. There is as yet no Russian Army establishment in Guinea, but a modern airfield, capable of taking the largest aircraft, has been built with the help of the Soviet Air Force. In conjunction with the airfield a meteorological service (headed by a Czech) has been organised and a Prague announcement has claimed that plans have been completed to extend this service to 'other African States.'

In September 1960, a further agreement was reached between Guinea and Russia for a submarine base. The existence of the agreement has been denied but twenty-five Russian submarine officers have since arrived and work on the base has started. This, incidentally, will give Russia her first submarine base in the Atlantic.

Ghana and Mali are Drawn in

The basis for Russia's military advance into Ghana was laid in 1960. The first real military liaison between Ghana and Russia started with the upheaval in the Congo and the subsequent mutual Ghanaian and Soviet wish for concerted military action to support first Lumumba and, after his death, Gizenga. Nkrumah was an invaluable ally for Russia in the resultant manoeuvrings.

One difficulty was that Ghana had in her armed forces several hundred British and Canadian officers whom Nkrumah apparently felt he could not trust. While it would have been diplomatically difficult for him to get rid of them outright, Nkrumah decided at least to counterbalance their influence by introducing Communist military personnel into his country. He did subsequently find a pretext to dismiss his British chief of staff and other British officers.

From the beginning of 1961 co-operation between the Soviet Army and the Ghanaian Army developed rapidly, starting with an invitation from the Soviet Ministry of Defence to Ghana to send a military delegation to Russia. Led by Brigadier S. J. A. Otu (who has since become chief of staff), the delegation arrived in Moscow in April 1961. Marshal Malinovsky gave a luncheon in its honour and a special reception was attended by, among others, Marshals Malinovsky, Zakharov, Rokossovsky, Chuikov and Admiral Gorshkov.

As guests of Air Marshal Rudenko, the Ghanaians attended an aerobatics display in their honour and further entertainment followed at the Frunze Military Academy, the Higher Combined Arms Command Training Establishment, the Frunze Higher Naval School at Leningrad and the Soviet Army Museum. Following this visit, Ghana announced, in September 1961, her intention of sending 400 military cadets to Russia for training by the Red Army.

Russia has not yet succeeded in extending the activities of the Soviet Air Force from Guinea to Ghana, but has done the next best thing by getting a strong foothold in Ghanaian civil aviation. In the middle of 1961 Ghana bought some Ilyushin 18 aircraft from Russia. These were delivered complete with 350 Russian crew and technicians to serve with Ghana Airways. Simultaneously 184 Ghanaians were sent to Russia to begin a five-year training course as pilots, navigators, radio operators and aircraft engineers.

It must be remembered that Ghana's only airline is very small. The number of Soviet crew and technicians placed at Ghana's disposal is therefore quite out of proportion to the needs of Ghana Airways and it can be assumed that they are not all from *Aeroflot*, the Russian State airline, but in fact from the Russian Air Force. Similarly, the number of Ghanaians sent to Russia for air training is more than Ghana Airways can readily absorb. A cover-up, so as not to alarm the West, must be suspected, particularly as so few details have been announced, the news leaking out bit by bit.

In September 1961 it became known that Czechoslovakia had undertaken to build a light weapon and ammunition factory in Ghana.

Mali's main military link with the Soviet bloc is also concerned with flying. Air Mali is even smaller than Ghana Airways, but operational control of it is now partly in Russian hands. Its Malian personnel, previously trained by France, are being retrained, in relays, in Czechoslovakia and Russia.

In the middle of 1961 a Czech airliner on the regular Prague-Bamako service crashed in North Africa, killing seventy-two persons. Papers found on the dead disclosed that twenty-four of them were instructors from the Soviet Air Force. Shortly before the crash Russia had promised Mali twenty-two aircraft, of which only twelve were believed to be earmarked for Air Mali. It is assumed that the other ten were intended as the nucleus of an air force and the Soviet instructors in the crashed airliner are similarly assumed to have been destined for this air force. They have no doubt been replaced.

There is no evidence of any Communist link yet with the Malian ground forces. As Mali is fairly remote and in any case inaccessible by sea, she would not be of great value to the Communist bloc as an army base. It is therefore logical to concentrate on her as a potential air base.

An African 'High Command'

The advantages of having military links with a few individual countries will be overshadowed when the 'African military high command' of the Casablanca group becomes a reality. Russia wholeheartedly supports the step, but one of the practical difficulties is the rivalry and jealousy within the group, with Nkrumah and Nasser both intent on being the dominant personality in control. Progress is therefore slow, but there is much Communist bloc pressure behind the scenes and in due course something of substance will no doubt emerge.

As this 'African high command' is intended for the specific purpose of interfering in the affairs of other African States, it could become a dangerous threat to the security of emerging countries which pursue a moderate policy. For that reason, it will not be able to rely on much material support from Western nations. Britain, for instance, can be expected to watch carefully to see for what purpose Ghana uses arms supplied by her.

The Casablanca group will therefore inevitably be driven to the Communist bloc for equipment and training. This is the opportunity for which Russia is waiting (a fact which has slightly dampened Nasser's enthusiasm). A five-nation command in Africa ready and eager for close co-operation with the Soviet bloc is a prize which even Russia could not have dreamt of as recently as 1959.

There is little the West can do to counter it.

Clandestine Supplies

Disturbing as these developments are and much as Western statesmen should ponder the problem, the more immediate physical danger to large parts of Africa lies in the Soviet bloc's unofficial, clandestine supply of military equipment and other aid to extremist movements and terrorists.

In the last three years Communist bloc arms, usually of Czech manufacture, have been found everywhere in Africa where there has been an organised outbreak of violence on a significant scale.

I have written earlier about the supply of Czech arms to Angola. It is therefore not necessary to refer to that again,

except to point out that the breakdown in supplies which
hampered Holden Roberto, the terrorist leader, would not
have occurred if events in the Congo had not prevented the
flow of goods from the Eastern Province, where Gizenga was
established, to the northern Angola border.

There were enough Communist-supplied arms and ammunition in the Congo's Eastern Province to meet Roberto's
immediate needs, but as Gizenga was then in a state of semi-
war with both Katanga and the Leopoldville group, there was
no way of transporting some of them to Angola at the critical
moment.

Arms for the Congo

The Congo is, admittedly, an exceptional case, but a look at
the method of supplying Communist arms to that tragic
country is worth while. There is an incorrect belief that no
arms reached the Congo from Communist sources before
independence in the middle of 1960. I was in the Congo at the
time and personally inspected many crates of new Czech
rifles and small arms ammunition in tribal villages, particularly
in the more remote parts of the north-east.

So far as I could discover at that time they had been brought
through Uganda, either from the Sudan or by the more
difficult route from Ethiopia. In Uganda, the police kept a
special watch for possible gun-running but failed to detect any.

The period between January 1960, when the Congo's coming independence was announced, and the end of June when
it became a fact, was an extremely busy time for the Communist bloc. It was not at the time foreseen what an utter
disaster independence would become, and intensive preparations were made for a conventional struggle – conventional on
the pattern of Cameroun, if necessary.

The Belgian Communist Party was a great help. While the
independence negotiations were still in progress in Brussels the

Belgian Communist Party got in touch with Lumumba and several of the other delegates from the Congo. It is now known that Lumumba and five of his future Ministers there and then sold out to the Belgian Communist Party which was acting as a go-between for the Soviet Embassy in Brussels. The five Ministers were Gizenga, Bisukiro, Ilunga, Kashamura and Mwamba. Gizenga was in fact whisked off to Prague for a while.

Between February and June, 125 selected Congolese were taken to Czechoslovakia and East Germany for intensive training in guerrilla warfare. During the same period a number of East Germans and Czechs arrived in the Congo, unknown to the Belgian authorities. They were to act as advisers in the so-called inter-party struggle for the coming elections which became a preparation for tribal warfare.

By the time independence arrived, fighting was in progress in many areas. True, it was tribal warfare which would probably have started in any case, but tribes which supported those political parties which had entered into an agreement with the Communists had at their disposal not merely the usual spears, but some modern weapons manufactured in Czechoslovakia. These parties included Lumumba's *Mouvement National Congolais*, Gizenga's *Parti Solidaire Africaine*, Kashamura's *CEREA* and the *ABAZI*.

The only force which perhaps could have maintained some degree of law and order was the Belgian-officered *Force Publique*. But within a few days of independence there was a Lumumba-condoned mutiny against the Belgian officers which destroyed this force overnight as a security instrument. All that remained to be done was to help Lumumba extend his dubious authority over the whole battlefield which was what most of the Congo had become. Russia immediately tried to place some means at his disposal.

The United Nations 'presence' had by then arrived and was

not behaving to Lumumba's or Russia's satisfaction. The United Nations had also passed a resolution that all aid for the Congo should be channelled through its contingent in the Congo. In spite of this fifteen Ilyushin 14 troop transport planes were flown from Russia to the Congo and handed over to Lumumba, complete with crews. Each aircraft also carried twelve Russians and a consignment of automatic rifles.

In defiance of an outright United Nations ban the aircraft were used to ferry pro-Lumumba troops to the Kasai front to help subjugate hostile forces.

He was also presented with 100 Russian three-ton trucks with the necessary maintenance staff. These trucks had been requested by the United Nations for its own troops, but on their arrival Russia withheld them from the United Nations and they, too, were used to transport Lumumba's troops to the Kasai front.

By the end of August, apart from the equipment and arms delivered, about 100 Russians and 125 nationals of other Communist States were in Lumumba's service. These figures do not include the more than 200 Russian and Czech 'diplomats' who were by then busy in the Congo.

After Lumumba

Then, suddenly, Lumumba's fortunes changed. He was ousted by his opponents and eventually killed. Gizenga now became the Communist front man. He fled to Stanleyville and there set up his own regime which held sway over the Eastern Province and parts of the Kivu and Katanga provinces. This was immediately recognised by the Communist bloc, and the Russian and Czech Embassies, expelled from Leopoldville after the fall of Lumumba, were reopened in Stanleyville, accredited to Gizenga's Government.

The Stanleyville area was already fairly rich in Communist arms, but fresh supplies were now organised to enable Gizenga to equip a proper army. This attempt met with only partial success.

Large deliveries of weapons could not be made as the Sudan courageously refused to give transit facilities to aircraft carrying any kind of material to the Congo except for delivery to the United Nations. That did not prevent smuggled supplies from Ghana and Guinea reaching the Stanleyville regime, but in smaller quantities. It also did not prevent Czech, East German and Russian military advisers being placed at Gizenga's disposal. And it did nothing to reduce the number of Congolese who were being sent by Gizenga for military training in Czechoslovakia and East Germany.

In August 1961 a half-hearted reconciliation took place between Gizenga and the Leopoldville Government of Adoula, Gizenga agreeing to become Deputy Prime Minister under Adoula. Moscow then claimed, by means of some peculiarly involved reasoning, that the creation of the Adoula Government had invalidated the idea that all outside aid to the Congo must be channelled through the United Nations.

Moscow Radio also claimed that Adoula's Government, having been confirmed by Parliament as the successor of Lumumba's first Central Government, was bound 'to operate all decisions previously made by Lumumba's Government.' These decisions included willingness to accept direct military aid from Russia.

When Adoula refused to act on this Soviet suggestion he was severely criticised as an imperialist stooge and Moscow Radio commented that 'the fight for real independence' will have to be continued by Gizenga. Although Moscow did not break off diplomatic relations with the Adoula Government, military supplies continued to arrive in Stanleyville where Gizenga remained, in spite of having nominally joined the Leopoldville Government, until his ultimate arrest in January 1962.

The arms arriving in Stanleyville were earmarked for use against Katanga and the military advisers sent had the task of preparing for an invasion of Katanga and the expulsion of the Western mining interests. If the rich copper and tin mines could not be seized, then they were to be destroyed so as at least to deprive the West of this asset. As things turned out, the United Nations forestalled the planned invasion with a military operation of its own which had much the same effect.

The Cameroun Revolt

Communist participation in the bloody uprising in Cameroun has been no less sinister. Elsewhere I have explained the important role China played in the Cameroun insurrection, but Chinese participation came long after terrorism had started. Russia was in from the beginning, from the time the late Reuben Um Nyobe, founder of the terrorist wing of the *Union des Populations Camerounaises*, led the first outbreak of violence in the Bamileke Province in May 1955.

During that period, however, Russia was as badly organised for the supply of direct military aid as she was during the Mau Mau uprising in Kenya. The result was that although Nyobe was helped with advisers and given every encouragement, not much aid reached him in the form of arms and he had to rely on his own resources. After his death in a military operation in September 1958, and notably from about the middle of 1959, the position changed considerably. His successor, the late Felix Moumié, could engage in proper organised warfare with modern Czech weapons. This phase started six months before the country became independent.

Before succeeding Nyobe, Moumié had enjoyed a prolonged stay in Russia as the guest of the Soviet Government. He also attended a course in guerrilla warfare in Czechoslovakia and made arrangements for arms deliveries from the Lenin works in that country.

In 1959, after Guinea had broken with France and was becoming a forward Communist base, Moumié settled in Conakry. From that moment the Bamileke revolt changed completely in character. The arms from Czechoslovakia, combined with a far higher quality of leadership in the field, made an immediate and obvious impact and within nine months 7,000 square miles of Cameroun territory were under terrorist control.

The French Army, which stayed behind after independence at the request of the legitimate Government, found itself engaged in a war of savage bestiality fought with astounding military efficiency.

The death toll exceeded 5,000 in a remarkably short time, with civilian men, women and children the main victims, as seems inevitable in all civil wars. The war continued into 1960 without any sign of Chinese participation, and as time dragged on Camerounians who had been on military courses in Czechoslovakia and East Germany filtered back to assume leadership in the field.

By late 1960 it at last became clear that the Government forces, supported by the French Army, were gaining the upper hand. The Russians therefore decided to cut their losses and extricate themselves from a tricky situation (as they were to do some time later in Angola).

It was at this time that the Chinese, seemingly disgusted with Russian faint-heartedness in the face of adversity, stepped in.

Towards the end of 1960 Moumié died while on a visit to Switzerland. On his deathbed he claimed that French Rightwing extremists had poisoned him. Before he died, he was able to make new arrangements with Chinese representatives then in Switzerland. From then on the Chinese Embassy in Conakry took charge of the insurrection, and Camerounian terrorist leaders were given priority for military training.

I have already mentioned the special courses conducted for

Africans in China. The following is the syllabus of one such course held specially for Camerounians between June and early August 1961.

PART I

(This part of the course took place at a military engineering school outside Peking.)

Explosives and Sabotage

June 21   Demonstrations of explosives and grenades.
     22   The classification of explosives and grenades.
     23   Detonators and fuses.
24/27   The correct use of explosives.
     28   Planning a sabotage operation.
29/30   Using explosives against houses, rails, bridges, tanks, guns, lorries, tractors, diesel engines and aeroplanes.

July   1   Revision and examination.
     2   The manufacture and application of explosives, including those made from easily obtainable materials.
     3   Home-made incendiaries and smoke bombs.
     4   Night operations.
     5   The manufacture and use of mines.
     6   The manufacture and use of grenades.

PART II

(Held at the Military Academy.)

Weapon Training and Military Strategy

July 12/16   Training in the use of semi-automatic rifles and carbines and the stripping down of rifles. (The students left the Academy on July 17th to return to Peking via Tientsin.)

July 18 'Imperialist weapons' – demonstrations and instruction in the use of the Colt and Browning revolvers, M 1918 and Browning sub-machine guns and mortars.

21 The theory and practice of guerrilla warfare.

22 Combat tactics.

23/24 Guerrilla methods.

25/26 Ambushes.

27 Entrenchments and the fortification of villages, attacks on communications, anti-tank and aircraft tactics.

PART III

Political Studies

July 28 'The Chinese Revolutionary Struggle' (lecture by Colonel Shou).

30 'The Democratic Revolution' (mobilisation of the peasants).

August 1 'The People's War.'

2 'The Party.' (In the captured notebooks, the party appears as the U.P.C. and it seems to have been the lecturer's intention to identify the U.P.C. with the Communist Party in the students' minds.)

3 'The United Front.'

4 'The imperialists are only paper tigers.' (The Communists must prevail by sheer weight of numbers.)

5 The establishment of revolutionary bases in rural areas.

6 The organisation of the Army.

I shall not dwell longer on Chinese intervention in a chapter which is concerned with Soviet military aid to Africa.

Training at Bernau and Houstka

Several references have been made to military training given to Africans in Czechoslovakia and in East Germany. The Czechs give the training at a special 'School for Partisans' at Houstka, twenty miles north-east of Prague on the River Elbe. The East German training establishment is at Bernau, near Dresden.

Candidates for training at these two establishments are recruited from African students already studying behind the Iron Curtain as well as from militant Africans in the various African countries. As in the case of ordinary students, free transport, all material needs and a cash allowance are provided. Keen rivalry exists between the East German and Czech institutions.

Obviously, less is known about clandestine military training and supplies of arms than about other Communist bloc activities in Africa, as no information on this subject is given by Communist sources. It is nevertheless known that Africans from as far away as Rhodesia, Mozambique, Angola and South Africa have been trained during the past two years. How many, however, is not known, but as the training courses continue all the year round the number of innocent-looking Africans who are in fact highly skilled in the use of modern weapons and in guerrilla warfare tactics must be steadily increasing.

After they complete their training the Africans normally return to their countries of origin, usually by underground routes, where they make themselves as inconspicuous as possible in order not to arouse suspicion. They may become once more ordinary farm workers or street sweepers, house servants or bus conductors. But they are ready and available in case of need if Moscow should decide to draw on their services.

Few of them are earmarked for important political roles.

The really promising are selected from those in Czecho-slovakia and East Germany for two and a half years' further training in Russia. These are destined for future political work. When the time comes for both moderates and genuine African nationalists to be replaced, the new leaders will in many cases be drawn from those who have completed this special training in Russia.

Just how well the ground is being prepared for the ultimate struggle, in case Africa cannot be won by non-violent means, time will show. One aspect must not be overlooked: Africans themselves will be fighting Russia's battle for her.

10

THE SATELLITES ARE USEFUL

If China is assisted in Africa by Vietnam's association with the former French territories, Russia is helped even more by the East European satellites.

Poland, Hungary and Bulgaria are making efforts to get into Africa by providing aid, though on a limited scale, 'experts' and even genuine technicians, but they have made no major impact yet.

East Germany and Czechoslovakia are in quite a different class and have become useful spearheads for Soviet infiltration. East Germany has a natural advantage over the rest of the Communist bloc States. She benefits from Germany's erstwhile close association with Africa, from the fact that many non-Communist Africans hardly know that there are today two Germanys, from having educational institutions which have a great appeal for genuine African students, from having a language which is an asset to any African who has mastered it and from Germany's war record which makes her military advisers much sought after.

East Germany is handicapped by the fact that West Germany has successfully established formal relations with all the new African States. The German Federal Republic has much to offer in terms of both aid and trade, but makes formal recognition of East Germany by any State – African or otherwise – a disqualifying condition.

This condition has so far been absolutely effective; no new

African State, not even Guinea, has dared to establish diplomatic relations with East Germany.

East Germany is therefore forced to operate through the back door, by using front organisations or so-called non-official organisations – trade unions, universities, youth movements, and so on.

Lacking diplomatic relations with any African country, East Germany is left free to indulge in the most undiplomatic conduct, and to some extent this cancels out the handicap of not being formally recognised. It is possible for her (as it is for China) to maintain far closer contact with terrorist and extremist movements in countries which are already independent but have moderate Governments than it is for Russia, who has in most cases established diplomatic relations with the Governments concerned. In being available to do the really 'dirty' work, East Germany is thus extremely useful.

Czechoslovakia is equally useful, but in a different way. Unlike East Germany, she has no difficulty in establishing diplomatic relations anywhere, and her industrial and economic potential is impressive.

When Russia prudently prefers to remain in the background, if only for a period, Czechoslovakia therefore often takes on whatever task has to be carried out. Moreover, she can often do so without frightening the African country concerned and without causing panic in the West, because having Czechs around is somehow regarded as not quite so ominous as having Russians about. Czechoslovakia, for instance, did much of the groundwork to prepare the way for Russia to move into Guinea, and Guinea is not the only example.

In September 1960, the Mali Federation (of the former French Sudan and Senegal) broke up. The Sudan took the name of Mali Republic. Her leaders already had Communist sympathies and it was decided that she had to be ensnared as soon as possible, but also as painlessly as possible so as not to cause too much alarm among other former French territories. Czechoslovakia therefore paved the way.

The Federation collapsed on September 22nd, 1960. Within a few days of the break-up the Czech Government invited a Mali governmental delegation to Prague to explore the possibilities of economic and cultural co-operation. The invitation was accepted.

Within a month of the break-up an unspecified number of special scholarships were made available, through the Mali Ministry of Education, for students to enter Czech universities. The first batch of twenty-nine students arrived from Mali on November 5th.

By February Czech doctors and nurses were working in hospitals in Mali, and a Czech-supervised public health scheme for Mali was announced.

In February, too, the Mali State Secretary for Information was invited to Prague. He arrived at the head of a delegation and during the talks that followed agreement was reached on co-operation in the fields of popular enlightenment and information.

Before February had ended the Czech airline, C.S.A., had extended its Prague – Conakry service to include Bamako, Mali's capital, and a Mali-Czech agreement had been signed under which the Czech news agency, *Ceteka*, would provide 'technical aid to the Republic of Mali for the establishment of her own news agency.' The formal announcement of this agreement was not made until May, during the all-African journalists' conference which had been convened under the auspices of the International Organisation of Journalists.

In Prague a delegation from Mali's Ministry of Communications had also agreed to allow Czechoslovakia to improve Mali's communication system. In early March it was agreed that Czechoslovakia would establish a leather processing factory in Bamako which when completed will produce each year one million pairs of leather shoes and 300,000 pairs of rubber shoes. In the middle of March an agreement was concluded under which Czech trucks and other transport equipment would be placed at Mali's disposal.

Much more has happened since then but I have chosen the first six months of Mali's separate existence to illustrate with what speed Czechoslovakia went to work. Each of the agreements signed made it necessary for a large number of Czech experts to go to Mali for a prolonged stay. Each expert had a clear-cut task to perform, so that within an incredibly short period Czechoslovakia was well established in Mali.

Russia had meanwhile remained in the background. She stayed there until the ground had been thoroughly prepared.

The same is happening in a number of other countries, but there is no need to dwell longer on this particular subject. If the point has been made that both Czechoslovakia and East Germany need special watching, then enough has been said.

11

'SOME LIKE-MINDED MARXISTS'

Africa is a continent of paradoxes. Nothing happens there according to the rules which apply in other continents. The sequence of cause and effect often appears to be entirely missing. Sometimes things seem simply to happen, or not to happen, in utter defiance of reason or logic. That must be accepted when trying to understand what has happened in Africa during the past three years since the Soviet offensive to replace the West began.

In all other continents there have been over the past forty years a large number of converts to the Communist cause. Yet nowhere has it been possible for them to gain sufficient power or influence to obtain actual control by normal means.

The Russian Army had to impose Communist rule on all the countries of Eastern Europe. In China a protracted war had to be fought and Communist rule came only after military conquest. The same applies to North Vietnam and will eventually probably also apply to Laos. I do not know Cuba but it is unlikely that the people of that island today have in Castro's Government the regime of their choice.

In Africa things are happening the other way round. Few Africans have become Communists. Moscow's own figure of 50,000 Communists in black Africa is not impressive among a total population of about 200 million. And yet, in spite of such a negligible success, which would have been most disheartening elsewhere, Russia's influence in Africa is increasing rapidly.

At the same time, while millions of Africans would like to maintain the closest contact with the colonial or former colonial Powers and are almost frantically anxious to retain the friendship and support of the West, the free world's sphere of influence in Africa is shrinking rapidly.

Whether the paradox is puzzling to Russia is impossible to say, but the policy-makers in Moscow have probably by now realised that they started off with one major misconception: the masses – the workers in the trade unions, the peasants and the so-called oppressed – are not nearly so opposed to the colonialists, and not nearly so ready to accept Moscow as a liberator, as was expected.

The true friends whom Russia is winning belong to the African intelligentsia. The Communist advance into Africa is, to Russia's surprise, not from below, but from above. Even the setting up of the All-African Trade Union Federation had to be rigged, and so visibly rigged that it disgusted many African trade unionists.

There are few genuine African workers' movements clamouring for solidarity with Russia. Yet Russia is well on the way to gaining full control of the African trade union movement. And in the long run it will not make any difference that she was able to do so only by means of manipulating minority groups whose connection with African workers can in many cases be seriously doubted.

It is even questionable how many of the so-called trade union and other leaders who have been ensnared by Russia into serving the Communist cause are Communists. Many of them are frustrated minor politicians who, for reasons of convenience, have allowed themselves to be built up by the Communist bloc. Often the reward has been simply money.

The truth is that many of them represent nobody but themselves. The reason why they can achieve so much is the depressing apathy of millions of Africans – apathy even in the alleged bitter struggle against colonialism and imperialism and an equal apathy about whether or not the Western colonialists are replaced by Communist colonialists. And the additional apathy in London and Washington.

An African Intelligentsia

In any event, the position in Africa now is that most of the allies of the Communist bloc – whether or not they are themselves rabid Communists – are not to be found among the genuine workers or proletariat, but among the more educated, many of whom are graduates of British, French or American universities. The turn of those now studying behind the Iron Curtain will come later.

Although these intellectuals, who are in most cases town or city bred, have grown away from the millions whose future will be most closely affected, they are the most outspoken leaders in the anti-colonial, anti-imperialist and anti-neo-colonialist struggle, and it is in this connection that Russia is best able to make common cause with them.

These Africans want political movements, political parties and 'action fronts' which can advance behind the shield of African nationalism, pan-Africanism or even Afro-Asian solidarity.

It is unlikely that Moscow is entirely happy about this development, but for the time being it is a situation which must be accepted – and if it must be accepted, then it also must be exploited. The future leaders now being trained behind the Iron Curtain will in due course have to build up mass movements from below. Meanwhile the various front organisations are doing the best they can to hold the fort. If, in the interim, there are to be political parties or political movements, then care must be taken that these are Left-wing movements.

The first public recognition of this development was in the statement on the Communist Summit in Moscow in December

1960, in a brief sentence which urged 'like-minded Marxists' to rally in the 'countries which have shaken off colonial tyranny and taken the path of independent development.'

The reference was clearly aimed at the new countries of black Africa. A closer look at the countries concerned throws further light on the Moscow statement. Wherever the transition from colonial rule to independence has worked relatively smoothly, control of the country concerned is vested in a political movement not yet penetrated by Communist-inclined intellectuals, and the opponents of the regime in power have not yet been organised into an effective opposition.

It therefore seems that Moscow, perhaps reluctantly, has decided that the third phase of the long-term policy can be successfully concluded in some countries only by making use of sympathetic intellectuals. This is the phase which calls for the dismissal or overthrow of African nationalist leaders who fail to come to terms with Moscow and who are either too independent-minded or who remain friendly with the West. By looking at Africa itself, the pattern falls into shape.

In considering this new development it is necessary in sub-Saharan Africa to distinguish between the former French and the British or former British territories. For this purpose the Congo can be classified with the former French territories. The Portuguese territories do not come into either of the two divisions, but as developments in them are in any case entirely different, I am not dealing with them here.

The distinction is necessary because the Africans in what used to be British Africa have until recently lived in comparative political isolation. The French territories, on the other hand, were closely linked with the political life of France herself, and Africans from these countries often took an active part in Metropolitan French politics.

Similar conditions did not exist in the Congo, where the

Africans had no organised political life. But there is a similarity between the former French territories and this former Belgian preserve. Both France and Belgium have vigorous and large Communist parties which play an important part in the national life of the two countries and which had close ties with ·Africa. In contrast, the British Communist Party is insignificant and never made an impact on British Africa. I am not referring to individual British Communists, but to the party as such.

Role of the French Communist Party

In France the Communist Party has at times participated in the Government of the country and in that capacity shared responsibility for ruling the then French territories. It is almost odd now to remember that during those periods the French Communists did not agitate for independence for French West or Equatorial Africa: anti-colonialism had not yet been discovered by Moscow. Instead, the French Communist Party worked for a more complete integration of the African territories into the national life of Metropolitan France.

If such a complete integration had taken place, then obviously French Communists, already exceptionally important in France, would have been greatly strengthened if they had powerful support in the African territories. Determined efforts were therefore made to get a strong Communist movement started in French Africa. But it was an effort to win support for the Communist Party in France, to strengthen its position in the overall French political struggle, and it was not then part of a Russian plan to extend Communism to Africa.

The most successful effort was in West Africa, where the *Rassemblement Démocratique Africain* (R.D.A.), in the nineteen-forties West Africa's most powerful political party, became little more than an offshoot of the French Communist

Party. But – and it must be remembered that we are dealing with Africa, the continent of paradoxes – the R.D.A. stood for an 'alliance between the French proletariat and the dependent peoples.' It did not seek independence; it wanted closer association with France for the African territories – and the French Communist Party fully supported these aims.

In the context of today's politics it seems another paradox that non-Communist Frenchmen, particularly those in Africa, saw something sinister, decidedly Communist, in the African desire to be more closely associated with France.

Felix Houphouet-Boigny, now President of the Ivory Coast and Moscow's 'enemy number one of African unity,' was the R.D.A.'s President. Then, as now, he stood for close association between France and Africa, and for that he was branded as 'Africa's Stalin.'

He was then a 'dangerous Communist' because he wished to cling to France. Today he is Moscow's enemy because he still wants to be associated with France. His political consistency contains a moral which should make many Europeans blush.

However that may be, through the medium of the R.D.A. the French Communist Party gained considerable influence in French Africa, particularly on the west coast.

But it was an influence based on an African belief that the French Union held out the greatest hope for their advancement. In due course, when political thinking everywhere became reversed, both the French Communist Party and the R.D.A. lost popularity in Africa for three reasons.

First, when the Communist line was suddenly changed to a condemnation of so-called colonialism and a demand for freedom and independence everywhere, the R.D.A. found it difficult to go along. Second, when African nationalistic thought in French Africa turned against France, the R.D.A.

was suddenly no longer regarded as Communist; it became instead a symbol of French imperialism and lost much of its standing. And, third, the change of policy by the French Communist Party was a bit drastic, even by African standards, and the party itself lost the confidence of many African leaders.

In passing it may be noted that according to French thinking in the years after the end of the Second World War, Guinea was the ideal – she was content to be 'separate' and had no troublesome thoughts about becoming more closely associated with Metropolitan France.

Curb on French Communists

Nevertheless, through its previous African endeavours, the French Communist Party had built up close connections with French Africa and in three territories in particular political movements remained under its wing. The movements were the *Parti Démocratique de Guinée*, the *Union Soudanaise* of what is today Mali, and the *Union des Populations Camerounaises*. The first of these three successfully led the Guinean move to break with France in 1958, the second has since successfully brought Mali within the Soviet sphere in Africa, and the terrorist branch of the third has been trying to overthrow the Cameroun Government ever since the country became independent in January 1960.

There is, however, evidence that for several years after the change of policy the French Communist Party was discouraged from attempting to extend its activities and influence in Africa. It has been suggested that Moscow had in fact forbidden it to do so during the late nineteen-fifties when it was Russia's definite policy not to work through African political parties. Whether that is true or not, it certainly is a fact that French Communists trod warily in Africa during the period when Moscow was studying Africa, working out policy and deciding that Africa was not ready for a struggle between political parties.

But since the Moscow statement about the desirability of 'like-minded Marxist' groups getting together in Africa, there have been signs of renewed activity.

Raymond Guyot, of the Central Committee of the French Communist Party and its expert on Africa, has frankly admitted this renewed activity.

'In recent years,' he said in a report to the Central Committee, 'Africa has stepped into the forefront of world politics. It is destined to play, and is beginning to play, a growing role in international relationships. Every country on this continent, with its population of over 250 million, is being caught up in the irresistible movement for independence, which is the typical feature of our times.

'. . . It is necessary above all to explain through our Press the problems posed by the new situation in Africa; to explain that the just struggle waged by the Africans and Malagasy pursues the same aims as our struggle, being directed against the same exploiters and oppressors; we should throw light on the attempts of the present rulers to retard the liberation of these people, and show the consequences with which these attempts are fraught.

'In the new situation we should establish contact, especially personal contact, with the African people, parties, organisations and their representatives, who can count on the effective solidarity of our working classes and our Party . . .

'The dissemination of Communist ideas in the African countries is at once the duty and task of our Party . . . We should aid the Marxist groups springing up in Africa, help in their educational work and, when the conditions arise, in forming parties there which would conduct their activities in the spirit of Marxism-Leninism.'

This should not be regarded as a new policy; it is more in the nature of a makeshift manoeuvre to collect on the swings what may be missed on the roundabouts.

Three Marxist Movements

In the former French territories much effort is now concentrated on a movement called the *Parti Africain de l'Indépendance* (P.A.I.). Formed in Dakar in 1952, it extended its membership to other French territories, but remained of little consequence throughout the nineteen-fifties. Since 1960 its value as a movement which can be used by the Communist bloc has greatly increased, especially as it was banned in Senegal in June of that year and went underground.

Several of its members – teachers, doctors, lawyers, but few 'workers' – have since been invited to Moscow and it is certain that funds have been placed at their disposal. It seems that Moscow only began to take P.A.I. seriously as a potential pro-Communist group when it became evident that the governments of Senegal and several other former French territories were rejecting the anti-Western line which was by then becoming fairly general in new Africa.

But as the P.A.I. has been turned into a subversive organisation, little publicity is now given to its activities and it is difficult to determine how strong and effective it is as a political instrument, and whether it is in fact making headway outside Senegal.

Apart from the P.A.I., a few other, smaller movements are also attempting to organise 'like-minded Marxists' in former French Africa into a recognisable and coherent body. One is called the *Parti de la Révolution Socialiste du Benin*. It concentrates its activities in the two small countries on the Bay of Benin, Togo and Dahomey, but its size and influence are also difficult to determine. It, too, appears to have little working-class support.

Further south the *Parti de l'Unité Gabonaise* is busy rally-ing 'like-minded Marxists' astride the Equator. The declared aim of this embryo movement is to break what links still exist with France and to bring Gabon in line with Guinea.

These movements are of a kind which only exists in former French territories, where there is more sophistication and where the French intellectual influence over a long period has produced a number of Africans who *can* be called Marxists. Today they have a political haven in Guinea and Mali, but how influential they may eventually become can only be a matter for speculation – in Moscow as elsewhere.

One consideration about them which cannot please Russia is that the genuine Marxist inclination which exists is the out-come of French Left-wing or, in other words, European influence. European influence of any kind is not desirable in Africa in the Soviet view: if these African intellectuals have absorbed their Marxist thinking from the French Communist Party then it is safe to assume that they have absorbed much else from France as well.

It means, furthermore, that they probably have ideas of their own regarding the future of Africa, ideas which do not necessarily coincide with Moscow's views – they may, for instance, merely want a truly Socialist Africa, which does not go nearly far enough for the Soviet Union.

Buying Congolese Leaders

The Congo, in contrast, absorbed little of Belgium's political and cultural sophistication during the seventy years of Belgian rule. Education in the Congo was in any case minimal, and nothing which can be vaguely called an intelligentsia really exists. The many political parties which mushroomed in the few months before the Belgians went (more than 200 partici-pated in the elections on the eve of independence) did not deceive the Russians into believing that orderly party-political rule was coming to the Congo.

The Soviet approach has therefore been straightforward throughout: to buy as many of the Congo's political leaders as possible and to assume that their tribes would fall in line behind them.

But there came a moment when it seemed advisable for Moscow to think again. That was in September 1961 when a kind of conciliation took place between the Leopoldville and Stanleyville regimes. There was just a chance that the new Adoula Government, in which Gizenga was to be Deputy Prime Minister, might settle down and become a normal government.

In that case a danger was that strong Western pressure might induce it to become genuinely neutral. It therefore became advisable to prepare some form of reserve political force to plot against the Government if the need should arise. As Gizenga was to be in the Government, he was not the right man to lead the new group.

It is fairly certain that the man picked for this role is Anicet Kashamura, of the *Cerea* party in the Kivu Province. Kashamura is one of the few Congolese who understand Marxism, and he is an avowed Marxist. He has spent some time in both Russia and in Communist China and has for long been in close touch with the Belgian Communist Party.

Kashamura was Minister of Information in Lumumba's Government and had been one of the future Ministers who at the time of the Brussels negotiations committed themselves wholeheartedly to prepare the way for Russia in the future independent Congo. After Lumumba's fall he joined Gizenga in Stanleyville but subsequently quarrelled with him and for a short period set up his own Communist regime in the Kivu Province. At the time of writing attempts are being made to arrest him.

New Movement in Nigeria

In the former British territories it has been appropriately in Nigeria that the first self-styled Marxist group has appeared – appropriate because of the pro-Western views and anti-Communist policy of the Prime Minister, Sir Abubakar Balewa.

Called the Nigerian People's Party, it had an obscure beginning sometime in the middle of 1961 when it published a pamphlet called 'The New Nigeria.' Care was taken not to make the pamphlet available outside a limited, selected circle.

The pamphlet gives the aims of the party as 'uniting, organising and guiding the Nigerian people in their battle for a better life, a hopeful future and for the triumph of Socialism in Nigeria.' There are references to the 'ravages' left by colonialism and the 'misery and poverty' of the people. Corruption and dishonesty, it claims, still dominate daily life and the peasants and workers are reduced to a 'life of degradation.'

Students, it goes on, are deprived of the benefits of a 'democratic and scientific' education while people engaged in the professions or in commerce have no chance of improving their lot as industry and commerce are in the hands of foreigners.

'Neo-colonialist forces' are attempting to destroy independence, and 'imperialists and British colonialists continue to dominate and exploit us,' it declares. In spite of independence, the army, the police, public services, the liberal professions and industry continue, according to 'The New Nigeria,' to be directed by foreigners who allegedly do not act in the interests of the country.

The pamphlet describes the Nigerian People's Party as 'a revolutionary patriotic mass party, born from historic conditions to guide and direct the Nigerian people in their fight against imperialism, feudalism, through the consolidation of independence and the national dignity of the Nigerian nation towards a richer and better life of peace, harmony and progress.'

Among the other things the N.P.P. stands for are a united Nigeria 'without regionalism and with a republican regime.' Parliament is to be elected by universal suffrage by all over the age of sixteen. The means of production are to be nationalised and a 'national plan' drawn up. All mineral resources are to belong to the State and foreign trade must become a State monopoly.

Also: 'In those parts where property is owned communally, it will be so preserved to form the basis for co-operatives.' Agricultural co-operatives will be developed throughout the country and only Nigerians will be allowed to own land. Land now belonging to foreigners will be taken over by the State. And much more.

The pamphlet bears the imprint of the Nigerian Trade Union Congress (the Russian sponsored movement which has broken away from the T.U.C. of Nigeria) which represents about one-third of Nigeria's unions. This is significant because not one of Nigeria's three main political parties has shown obvious leanings towards Moscow. True, the Action Group and the National Council of Nigeria and the Cameroons are both much more militant than the Prime Minister's Northern People's Congress and many fighting nationalistic speeches have come from them, but they appear to be wary of overtures from the Communist bloc.

Not so, however, a curious group of young and on the whole educated Nigerians (sponsored by the World Federation of Democratic Youth) who call themselves the Nigerian Youth Congress. It seems probable, therefore, that 'like-minded Marxists' from the Youth Congress and the Nigerian T.U.C. have come together to form the rather vague Nigerian People's Party, which is not a political party but quite plainly a movement of the kind which Russia has now decided should be encouraged as a precautionary measure.

The fact that it made its appearance in Nigeria should not

escape notice. Nigeria is in population (approaching forty million) the largest country in Africa and potentially one of the most influential.

There is also in Northern Nigeria a self-styled Communist Party of Nigeria, but not even Moscow appears to pay attention to it. It is simply a group of ambitious young men who could not think of a better name. Its influence and standing are nil at present.

Other Examples

In Sierra Leone, one of the most recent and smallest of the former British territories to attain independence, there are signs that part of the All-People's Congress, at present the opposition party, is organising itself into a Marxist group with Soviet affiliations. That does not mean that it is as yet a Russian-backed Communist group, but in the absence of anything more concrete for Russia to lay her hands on, it has, it seems, been decided to attempt to win its allegiance.

In the Horn of Africa Moscow has been fortunate in finding, probably to its own surprise, the nucleus of an actual Communist Party in Somalia. Although Somalia is one of Africa's most undeveloped territories and can make little claim to have an intelligentsia, there is an explanation for this otherwise surprising fact.

The reason is three-fold. First, the largest part of the present Somalia is the former Italian Somaliland which remained under Italian administration after the Second World War as a United Nations Trust territory. During this latter period, which lasted until the middle of 1960, the Italian Communist Party was a formidable force in Italy. Although the Italian administrators tried hard to proscribe its influence, the Italian Communists succeeded in building up an active nucleus in Somalia.

Second, French Somaliland adjoins Somalia. Although a small territory, French Somaliland is relatively much more prosperous than the other Somali-inhabited areas, with a higher standard of education, and for a time it had the attention of the French Communist Party. Some of this influence rubbed off on the small number of educated Somalis to the south.

Third, Egypt has for long taken a close interest in Somali affairs. For at least two years before independence a permanent Somali 'delegation' lived in Cairo. It represented Somali extremists, but one of its tasks was to arrange for young Somalis to be educated in Egypt. It also managed to get a number into Iron Curtain educational institutions.

The three influences working together resulted in a number of Communist cells being formed in Somalia before independence. The cells never developed into an official Communist Party but they did succeed in getting the teachers organised into a trade union, and the teachers are the main group in Somalia which can claim to constitute an intelligentsia.

Somalia is perhaps the only country in Africa where Moscow has acknowledged the improbability of imposing its influence at this stage from below rather than from above. The link between this Somali group and Moscow is therefore not, as elsewhere, mainly a precaution. It is becoming the main channel of communication.

Tanganyika and Kenya

In Tanganyika Julius Nyerere's attitude towards co-operation with the West has proved highly irksome to Moscow. The country's trade union movement, however, has a militant anti-West wing with which the W.F.T.U. has made contact and which is already exerting pressure. In part this pressure contributed to Nyerere's decision to resign as Prime Minister.

The Communists' problem is how to foster political leadership which is more in accord with the thinking of militant trade union leaders. Moscow believes it has found the answer in Zuberi Mtemvu, a young African who leads the extremist but as yet small African National Congress of Tanganyika.

Since independence Mtemvu has been fêted behind the Iron Curtain and in China, and he has been given funds to help him seek out 'like-minded Marxists' in Tanganyika who can be formed into a nucleus for political action when the opportune moment arrives.

The situation in Kenya is more complicated. Kenyatta was in close touch with the British Communist Party while studying in Britain. He also visited Russia, but there was for long uncertainty about whether he was a practising Communist. In any case, he had to watch his step for a long time.

During his many years in prison and as a restricted person, after being convicted of managing the Mau Mau, Kenyatta could in any case not keep in touch with Moscow. Oginga Odinga, a close associate of Kenyatta, became the Communist mouthpiece. Odinga is not by a wide margin in Kenyatta's intellectual class but he is useful for whatever work the Communists want done, especially as he is a member of the Legislative Council.

He has travelled extensively behind the Iron Curtain and in China, and has managed to arrange for the supply of funds from both Moscow and Peking. Lately he has also been receiving money from the Afro-Asian Solidarity Fund.

When Kenyatta eventually, in 1961, regained full freedom, a fairly effective Communist group had already been organised by Odinga within the Kenya African Nationalist Union, and it was relatively rich. Odinga has remained in control of this group.

Tom Mboya, at the time of writing still secretary-general of the party, has no links with Moscow. He is, moreover, the influential leader of the Kenya Federation of Labour which is affiliated to the West's International Confederation of Free Trade Unions. A clash of interests between him and Kenyatta was inevitable and the outcome appears to have been that while Mboya has retained the leadership of the workers' movement, Kenyatta has become more closely identified with the Left-wing group led by Odinga.

Part of Mboya's labour movement is, however, getting restive and a split in the near future is likely. A strong Left-wing element has yielded to W.F.T.U. pressure and is in a state of near-revolt against Mboya's leadership. To save himself Mboya may decide to move to the Left.

The Communist drive, even at the so-called intellectual level, is steadily moving down Africa, from north to south. There is no evidence that the South African Communist Party is attempting to extend its influence northwards. Attempts to influence African thinking in Nyasaland and the Rhodesias come mainly through East Africa; in recent months the disruptive events in the Congo, especially since the rape of Katanga, have produced signs of efforts to influence the attitude of the Africans along the Northern Rhodesian copperbelt.

But Moscow is treating the current African Marxists with caution. Part of the reason is that too many of them have a strong leaning towards Tito and may well become dangerous Titoists themselves. Others – as is the case in Algeria and Cameroun – find Mao Tse-tung more to their liking.

12

THE WIDENING GULF IN AFRICA

Mutual jealousy, rivalry for leadership, absence of common interests or a common aim and vastly different customs and background have all contributed to the deep divisions which are developing in Africa. But the fact that the leaders within the rival groups are able to co-operate makes it obvious that the existence of rival factions is not entirely due to these reasons.

There are sub-divisions within the opposing groups, but of the two main blocs the one seeks generally to be neutralist while maintaining, with reservations, friendship with the West. The other is identifying itself more and more with the Communist bloc.

The first is known vaguely as the Monrovia group and the second as the Casablanca group. The Monrovia group developed out of what was previously called the Brazzaville group which comprised twelve of the former French territories. They decided in December 1960 at a meeting in Brazzaville to retain links with France. Subsequently, at a conference in Monrovia in May 1961, Liberia, Nigeria, Sierra Leone, Ethiopia and Tunisia established links with this group which appear to be durable.

The Casablanca group consists of Ghana, Guinea, Mali, Morocco and Egypt, and developments early in 1962 indicated that Libya and Somalia have also found a political haven in this group.

But the division is not as clear-cut as it appears on paper. In all the countries of the Monrovia group there are strong elements pulling vigorously towards the Casablanca Powers and this may lead to bitter internal strife in each one of them.

In addition, there is in Uganda, Kenya, Tanganyika, the Rhodesias and the Congo a deep division among the leaders in their respective wishes to become identified with one or the other of the two groups. In the Portuguese territories the extremists have won full recognition from the Casablanca group while the moderates look to the Monrovia bloc for support.

Rival Military Commands

On paper the Casablanca Powers have a unified military command, set up in August 1961, with headquarters in Cairo and an Egyptian general as overall commander. Ghana, supported by Guinea and Mali, is trying to get the headquarters moved to Accra, not only for reasons of Nkrumah's prestige or out of fear that Nasser will be able to exert too much pressure.

They argue that Egypt is too far away from the real arena of African conflict – which is Africa south of the Sahara where the 'imperialists,' 'neo-colonialists' and African 'stooges' who allegedly act as instruments for the imperialists are supposedly most active.

The high-command is, after all, meant to serve the interests of so-called *African* patriots, to be at their disposal whenever they should feel in need of help.

Although the command has the wholehearted support of the Communist bloc, it is not yet an effective force, partly because of the opposition to Cairo as a suitable headquarters. The objection to having an Egyptian general in command is less strong, as it is realised that Egypt is perhaps in a better position to provide an adequate general.

Within the Monrovia group, the twelve Brazzaville Powers (now known as the African and Malagasy Union) have also

concluded a defence pact and have established a joint defence
council with headquarters in Ouagadougou, the capital of the
Upper Volta Republic which adjoins Ghana. If the Casablanca group's military command should be moved to Accra,
the two rival military headquarters will be uncomfortably near
each other, the distance between the two capitals being a mere
500 miles of open country.

There are many responsible African leaders who see great
dangers in the development of two factions basically hostile to
each other, but efforts to bring about some kind of reconciliation have met with absolutely no success. One notable failure
was an effort by President Tubman of Liberia. He invited all
African States to a Summit conference in Monrovia towards
the middle of 1961.

It was hoped that if the leaders in the rival groups could
sit down together to discuss the many problems facing
emerging Africa, the political temperature and antagonism
might be generally reduced. But nothing came of this hope
– the members of the Casablanca group refused to attend,
which made relations between the two groups even
worse.

A second effort by Sir Abubakar Balewa of Nigeria to
achieve the same end at a conference convened in Lagos in
January 1962, failed equally dismally.

Communist attacks on the men ruling the Monrovia bloc
States, and particularly on those in control of the Brazzaville
group, are growing in intensity and bitterness, and the African
leaders under fire are becoming sensitive about the continuous
jibe that they are Western stooges and traitors to African
nationalism.

As a result there is a noticeable tendency on the part of
many of them towards a greater degree of non-alignment – of
less identification of themselves with the free world. This is by
itself an indication of the Soviet bloc's ability today to exert

direct pressure even on African governments hostile to the creeping Communist influence in Africa.

According to Moscow the Casablanca group is the 'only true expression of the aspirations of the African people,' and must be supported to the exclusion of all other considerations in the 'anti-imperialist' struggle.

Instead of trying to win over the support of those who now rule the Monrovia group, Moscow is encouraging the more extremist and militant politicians in opposition in the countries of this group and is advocating the eventual overthrow of the governments.

Personal Attacks

Plyshevsky himself has bitterly attacked the members of the Brazzaville group. 'The policies pursued in the world arena by some of the new African States,' he has written in the *World Marxist Review*, 'are not always in accord with the interests of their people. For example, Cameroun, Congo, Ivory Coast, Dahomey, Gabon, Upper Volta, Madagascar, Niger, the Central African Republic, Senegal and the Chad Republic obstructed the efforts of the Afro-Asian group . . . to uphold the interests of the Algerian national liberation movement . . .'

In the same article he wrote: 'It has been noted . . . that in many of the former French colonies and the trustee territories which have now become independent . . . the people are still denied the democratic rights they have fought for. Many fighters for independence have been thrown into prison or concentration camps, some by the colonialists, others by the newly established governments whose domestic policies are by no means democratic. The people often have no opportunity to voice their views on the state of affairs or openly to put forth their demands.'

And: 'The French colonialists hope to save at least part of their African possessions . . . In this they are aided by some local leaders who, fearing their own people, are ready to enter into political deals with the French Government in order to remain in the saddle. Typical of this is Felix Houphouet-Boigny, President of the Ivory Coast, who held the African Affairs portfolio in the French Cabinet in 1956. An inveterate supporter of the French colonialists, this man took it upon himself to persuade the political leaders of other former French colonies that it was in their interests to form a federation and enter into partnership with the West.

'According to the capitalist Press, Houphouet-Boigny urged the African countries voluntarily to abridge their freedom and ally themselves with their former colonial rulers. Other leaders of the same type are Abbot Fulbert Yuolou, President of the former French Congo, and Prime Minister Mamadou Dia of Senegal . . .'

In an attack on the moderate Cameroun leadership Plyshevsky has written: 'This former French trustee territory became an independent State, the Cameroun Republic, on January 1st, 1960. In reality it is an African province of France under a treaty signed before independence by the Cameroun authorities . . . On the basis of bilateral agreements, France has military bases on Cameroun territory. Freedom fighters are still kept in prison. Some administrative posts in the republic are occupied by foreigners. Because of this, the people of the formally independent Cameroun are forced to continue guerrilla war . . .

'This is not the kind of independence that the people fought for. It may be acceptable to Prime Minister Amadou Ahidjo, who is connected with the French ruling circles, but certainly not to the people. It is understandable, therefore, that although the Government of the Cameroun Republic has a seat in the United Nations, the people do not feel they are independent and are continuing the national liberation struggle.' (Ahidjo is, of course, President, not Prime Minister.)

Official Soviet writing abounds with such personal attacks on the leaders now in office in countries of the Brazzaville bloc. Similar attacks are now starting against the leaders in office in former British territories who feel themselves drawn towards this group, such as Julius Nyerere, Sir Abubakar Balewa, and even the more moderate leaders of Kenya, such as Robert Ngala, head of the Kenya African Democratic Union.

As has been noted, these attacks are slowly but surely beginning to make an impact, particularly as it is daily becoming more clear that the Soviet bloc has no longer any wish to come to terms or even to establish friendship with the African leaders who have won independence but who have adopted policies of moderation.

Collapse of the Mali Federation

In the former French territories a major set-back for the forces of moderation was the break-up of the Mali Federation (between Senegal and the former French Sudan). The background, briefly, is that when, in December 1958, leaders of the then French West African territories met to decide various aspects of their future, some were in favour of forming a federation among themselves to re-create, in a modern form, the old Mali empire which had played an important part in north-west Africa in the fourteenth and fifteenth centuries.

There were difficulties, partly because there was no agreement on what the proposed federation's attitude should be towards the then emerging pan-Africanism, towards so-called positive neutralism, relations with Russia, and a number of other subjects.

The Senegalese leaders, notably Leopold Senghor and Mamadou Dia, stood firmly against adopting cut-and-dried policies at such an early stage, especially as the tendency then was to break entirely with France and generally to adopt extreme attitudes – a tendency which they opposed.

The outcome was that that particular federation was never formed. Instead, a smaller federation consisting only of Senegal and the (French) Sudan came into being. This, however, took the name 'Mali.'

The undisputed ruler of the (French) Sudan was then already Modibo Keita, a Moslem who ruled his one-party State with a firm hand and who tended to seek guidance from the Arab world until, subsequently, he began to accept guidance direct from the Communist bloc. When the Mali Federation was formed, he became its Prime Minister. Mamadou Dia of Senegal became Deputy Prime Minister.

The two men had little in common and clashed from the outset. Keita wanted neutralism, Dia wanted friendship with France. Nevertheless, it seemed as if the Senegalese leaders would at least be able to prevent a decided swing to the Left in foreign policy, but within two months Keita was not only ignoring the wishes of his Senegalese partners but trying to gain control over the domestic affairs of Senegal as well.

The Senegalese leaders took the only way out – they broke away, ending the Federation. Senegal was now free to pursue her own policies, but at the same time Keita was also free to do what he liked with his own country, which became the Mali Republic. Senegal's restraining influence was gone.

How quickly Mali swung to the Left has already been mentioned. In fact, within twelve months there were established diplomatic missions in Bamako from Russia, Czechoslovakia, Poland, Hungary, Bulgaria, Communist China, North Vietnam, North Korea, and Mongolia. East Germany, not being allowed diplomatic recognition, has had to make do with an economic mission.

A Fifth Column

The break-up of the short-lived Mali Federation was followed by the much looser arrangement for co-operation between Senegal and the remaining States (excluding Guinea) which had formerly comprised West and Equatorial Africa, and that is certainly on the credit side. But the deep division in Africa which this has caused is beset with dangers and eventual warfare cannot be ruled out.

It is no good arguing that the Brazzaville group, with the allies it has in the Monrovia bloc, is numerically bigger than the Casablanca group. The latter has much more openly the unrestricted support of the Communist bloc than the Brazzaville group has of the West, even of France. Furthermore, a formidable pro-Russian or pro-Chinese fifth column already exists in each of the countries.

It is a fifth column which derives much support from the West, and not only from unofficial Western organisations. In their eagerness to woo all African politicians all the time, friend and foe alike, Western governments are doing a great deal to undermine the authority and strength of the Africa which is represented by the movements and governments of sanity and moderation.

The potential fifth column and the Casablanca bloc together are therefore assured of more support than the Brazzaville group and its potential allies can usually hope to muster.

The trend is unmistakable. In Angola the invaders received world-wide acclamation while those Africans who did not join the uprising were ignored. In Kenya Jomo Kenyatta and his extremist colleagues are today the heroes while the moderate Kenya Africans and the several million tribesmen who reject Kenyatta and all he stands for are dismissed as nonentities by most of the Western countries.

Only in Ghana, it seems, is the West slowly beginning to realise that there are Africans who are not Western stooges who object not only to Nkrumah's dictatorship but also to his drift into the Soviet camp.

In Nyasaland Hastings Banda's willingness to drift in the

same direction, given the chance, is ignored, as is the trend of utterances by some of the fire-eaters of Northern Rhodesia's United National Independence Party. Even about Antoine Gizenga in the Congo very few words of condemnation have been heard at the United Nations or, for that matter, in Washington or London.

The Brazzaville group has been thinking in terms of forming a united bloc at the United Nations and of becoming, with the other Monrovia Powers, a kind of pressure group. Opinion among the member States is not agreed on the desirability of such a move. Even if the plan is carried out the whole Monrovia group will represent merely eighteen votes in a General Assembly with 104 seats.

The argument that the Casablanca group does not command more votes is not valid. It can at all times rely on solid Communist bloc support, while the West, too timid to be decisive, is sure to leave the moderates in the lurch as often as not. And, though it hardly needs pointing out, the Federation of Rhodesia and Nyasaland has no seat at the United Nations.

No Commonwealth Bond

Although the jealousies and rivalries would probably in any case have caused deep divisions among the leadership of the new Africa, the opportunities the clashes have given the Communist bloc and the skill with which they have been exploited are bringing Africa steadily nearer the brink. A catastrophe of the greatest magnitude is possibly approaching – a catastrophe which could either set Africa ablaze or deliver most of it into Communist hands.

The extent to which Russia and China may then quarrel over the spoils will be no consolation either to the free world or to Africa. Once that stage has been reached, there will be nothing the West will be able to do to save not only the millions of innocent and moderate Africans but the African continent itself. It may be argued that the West will have deserved what it gets, but that certainly does not apply to the millions of non-fanatical Africans.

Until not long ago there was still a feeling that the Commonwealth would be a factor which could hold the former British Africa together, but that has proved to be a forlorn hope. The Commonwealth influence has not been of the slightest use in helping Nigeria and Ghana to overcome their mutual hostility. It has done nothing to lessen the vicious attacks by Ghana or even Tanganyika on the Europeans in Rhodesia, and has contributed nothing towards the efforts to find a solution to the racial problems of Rhodesia – a solution which would be fair to the European community and to the moderate Africans, and not only to the extremists.

One question, however, remains: Is it now too late, is the disaster inevitable? Or can something still be done to help Africa towards the future which most Africans desire?

13

STILL SOME GOODWILL

Although Russia's progress in Africa has not been smooth – and there are still many pitfalls ahead for her – the struggle for the world's second largest continent is gradually moving towards a climax. It must not be forgotten that the Communist leaders have remarkable staying power and are less discountenanced by set-backs than their counterparts in the West. Slowly but surely (and in some places not so slowly) world Communism is ferreting its way into all corners of Africa while the West looks on – sometimes with alarm and sometimes complacently.

What is far too often overlooked is that there is still in Africa a tremendous reservoir of goodwill towards the West. But instead of drawing on it, it is consistently ignored and discouraged. In the universal anti-colonialist passion which is sweeping the world, any African who does not rant loudly and repeatedly against the evils which the white man is said to have brought to Africa is regarded by the West as an oddity and by the East as a traitor to the cause, beneath contempt and, if he has any influence, to be undermined or overthrown.

Some rethinking could fruitfully be done. It is perhaps too much to ask that it should be done at the United Nations, but influential circles in Washington and London could try to learn that many sober Africans who get along well with white people are as truly African, often more so, than the demagogues who denounce and demand and attack without interruption. The United States in particular could consider whether she is not making dangerous common cause with the Russians in working against the interest of these Africans.

Many American and British idealists must learn that not all Africans share their revulsion and condemnation of colonialism and of the white man's record in Africa. Many Africans most decidedly do not believe that the history of colonialism is entirely bad, and even many who condemn the European role in Africa nevertheless feel that when Africa's future well-being is considered, anti-colonialism is no longer a practical issue.

President Ahidjo of the Cameroun Republic has said so bluntly. Referring to what he called the gratuitous statements about colonialism made at the Belgrade conference of neutralist leaders in September 1961, he declared: 'Anti-colonialism is outdated. Our task is now national construction.' Mamadou Dia, Prime Minister of Senegal, has phrased it differently: he has spoken of the 'withering anti-colonialism which is born of real political childishness.'

A Nigerian, Alfa Walli, writing in the Lagos newspaper *Daily Times*, has tried to point out to fellow Africans that 'the time now is not one for shouting colonialism and imperliasm' but for all Africans to consider the social, political and economic problems of their continent.

President Leopold Senghor of Senegal, one of Africa's greatest nationalist leaders, has written: 'Independence is not snatched from demagogic speeches and merely anti-colonial attitudes. It builds itself up patiently, day by day, by going beyond the denial of anti-colonialism with positive work in nation-building and international co-operation.' Of France he has said: 'The genius of France is essentially the genius of method, of research, of clarity and – what one very often forgets – a certain feeling of humanity.'

A Kenya African, J. P. Oleche, has written in a letter to the

East African Standard: 'What has been achieved by the European oligarchy is remarkably great and cannot be under-rated by the Africans even at the dawn of independence. Building a completely pagan, primitive and barbarous country into a semi-civilised nation within a space of sixty years is no easy job . . . Whether our own Government will equal what the British have done for us in the same time only experience will tell.' In the context of present-day politics in Kenya, this pronouncement must have required courage.

The former Nigerian firebrand, Dr Azikiwe, now Governor-General of his country, said on August 6th, 1961, the centenary of the cession of Lagos to the British Crown, that most Nigerians would agree that this event had produced good.

The *Daily Times* of Lagos, writing of Britain as Nigeria's 'former colonial master,' has commented: 'By far the greatest contribution of Britain, in the context of world politics today, is her heroic and unrelenting role to ensure that the world enjoys peace and security . . . The world must continue to look to Britain to turn to good account her strength and tested counsel which alone is the last and surviving hope for the regeneration of world peace and security.'

Also referring to Britain's rule in Nigeria, Sir Abubakar Balewa said on independence day while addressing departing colonial officials: 'Today we are reaping the harvest which you sowed and the quality of the harvest is equalled only by our gratitude to you . . . We are grateful to the British officers we have known, first as masters and then as leaders and finally as partners, but always as friends.'

Many similar statements are constantly made by Africans at all levels in the colonial and former colonial territories. They can be quoted in great numbers but they are seldom found in the newspapers. Only the political agitators are given head-lines.

Example of Barotseland

Many exceptionally prominent African leaders (although they are not necessarily politicians) are unhappy about the rapid withdrawal of European rule and some are frankly opposed to it. One example is the ruler of Barotseland, Sir Mwanawina Lewanika, who leads 300,000 people, most of whom are devoted to him. Barotseland is part of Northern Rhodesia, in the Central African Federation.

British rule in Barotseland began in 1891, when the ruler at that time, King Lewanika, voluntarily accepted British protection. The provisional agreement of that year was replaced in 1900 by a formal treaty recognising King Lewanika and his heirs as the undisputed kings of Barotseland with the right to negotiate direct with Queen Victoria and her heirs. (In 1902 King Lewanika attended the coronation of Edward VII as an honoured guest.) It was from Barotseland that British rule was subsequently extended to what is now Northern Rhodesia.

For more than sixty years relations between the Barotse and the Colonial Office, which supervised the administration, have remained extremely friendly.

Since the creation of the Central African Federation Barotseland has faithfully co-operated with the Federal Government. The son of the present king, Godwin Lewanika, is in fact a pro-Welensky member of the Federal Parliament. Barotseland is, moreover, an African territory which throughout the recent turbulent years has remained absolutely peaceful and calm.

But, as was to be expected, the rising African politicians in the rest of Northern Rhodesia have little sympathy for the rulers of Barotseland, and they are supported by a small number of Barotse who have left their homeland and are agitating from outside.

Their agitation is in a way understandable. King Mwanawina rules through a Council known as the *Kuta*, which traditionally consists of tribal elders and some members of the king's family. Individual members of the Council are responsible for the administration of specific regions of Barotseland. The system works well.

To become accepted as a tribal elder, eligible for service on the *Kuta*, an African must win the respect and trust of his community over a period of many years and he must prove that he is capable of giving leadership. Many of the Barotse who have left to become politicians, and who are now agitating for a change, have no hope of passing these traditional tribal tests.

They have therefore moved to Lusaka, the Northern Rhodesian capital, to join the United National Independence Party of that territory, led by Kenneth Kaunda, which demands that Barotseland be placed under the jurisdiction of a future African government which would control the whole of Northern Rhodesia, preferably independent of Britain.

The idea of an end to British rule at this stage is rejected outright by the Barotse leaders, and early in 1961 the King and some of his elders travelled to London to tell the British Government that they and their people want Barotseland to remain as a British Protectorate. The report of the Monckton Commission in 1960 made specific mention of the 'deep loyalty to the person of the Queen' that is prevalent in Barotseland.

The Barotse warning was straightforward. If the authority of Sir Roy Welensky's Federal Government is reduced, or if the Federation should collapse, and if Northern Rhodesia is placed under the control of African politicians who, in the Barotse view, do not represent the mass of Africans, then Barotseland will break away from Northern Rhodesia. The King and his tribal elders will then declare Barotseland to be a self-contained entity and, in terms of the treaty of 1900, the full recognition and protection of the British Government will be claimed.

If there must be a change, the Barotse argue, then it must be a slow and orderly transition, step by step and under British guidance. In the context of modern African politics such loyalty has become highly embarrassing for the British Government and the Barotse are today regarded by the Colonial Office as, paradoxically, obstructionists.

There are other examples. Uganda will be independent before the end of 1962, although the ruler of the biggest part of Uganda, the Kabaka of Buganda, with the support of his Parliament, has bitterly opposed the end of British rule before the many differences between his people and their neighbours in the other parts of Uganda have been peacefully settled.

In Kenya some of the tribes, such as the Masai and Somalis, do not want to be placed under an African government in Nairobi and would prefer British rule to continue. So would the twelve African tribes living in the coastal strip of Kenya. The 2,000-square-mile strip is leased from the Sultan of Zanzibar and does not form part of Kenya in spite of the economic integration that has taken place over the years. The British Government's viewpoint is that the twelve tribes must be handed over to the mercies of an African government in Nairobi if the agreement of the Sultan can be obtained.

Three Conditions for Success

President Bourguiba of Tunisia, whose nationalism has never been doubted, has said with reference to decolonisation: 'Experience has shown that the essential thing is not the expulsion of strangers, but the grasping of responsibility.' He has given three conditions which he regards as essential if decolonisation is to be a success. He places first the ability of the leaders taking over from the colonial rulers. Second comes the maturity of the people. Third is 'at least a grant-in-aid' from the departing colonial Power.

The United Nations and public opinion in both Britain and the United States appear to think only the last of the three qualifications is important, and Russia rules out all three.

The Congo is, of course, a classic vindication of Bourguiba's concept, but it is remarkable how many voices still place the blame for the Congo catastrophe on, in order of importance, 'imperialist' intrigue, 'neo-colonialism' (as practised by the *Union Minière du Katanga*, for example), 'mercenaries,' Belgium (for not having prepared the people better for independence), and, lately, Sir Roy Welensky.

Even today the maturity or ability of the mass of the Congolese politicians is seldom questioned. The only Congolese leader whose maturity, stability, patriotism and even sanity is seriously doubted appears to be Moise Tshombe, although those who know him (and I do) tend to believe that he represents an oasis of sanity in a desert of almost unrelieved barrenness.

Although the Congo is an extreme example, the fact remains that where the leaders are mature and able, the transition from colonial rule to independence stands a far greater chance of success.

The Communist and Afro-Asian demand is for all control to be handed over to the African communities irrespective of the state of development they have reached. This demand, which has powerful support at the United Nations as well as in Britain and the United States, is irresponsible.

Nobody pretends to maintain that the Africans in all territories are equally mature and responsible and have equally able leadership. Yet the demand continues, and Moscow never lets it rest, for the understandable reason that Communism has everything to gain if the Europeans who still retain a measure of control over a few areas in Africa drop everything and run.

People who believe that the process of decolonisation has in some cases been too rapid are not necessarily persons of ill-will towards Africans. They are not necessarily die-hard racialists: although some of them, of course, are. Many of them have Africa's interests truly at heart and may indeed be critical that more was not done sooner to prepare the Africans in some territories to assume more responsibility.

The fact remains that the impressive progress Russia has made in Africa within three short years has to a large extent been possible because of immature and opportunistic leadership in many of the African countries. That may soon include Kenya where European leadership has been successfully undermined by Moscow, London and Washington simultaneously. Whether the same will apply to the Rhodesias is still to be seen.

The Rhodesias

The advocates of an immediate transfer of power everywhere are not the only people of goodwill towards Africa and Africans. I should think that Leopold Senghor and Habib Bourguiba have every bit as much goodwill towards Africa as Kwame Nkrumah or Jomo Kenyatta.

The white population of Northern and Southern Rhodesia can still play an immense role if a serious effort is to be made to resist the spread of Soviet influence in Africa. They are by no means all bad people, but they need the support of the free world rather than the abuse they are now getting. On their side, people like Sir Roy Welensky could do more to control the undesirable racial elements in the country, both white and black. Extremism of any kind should be more firmly controlled.

A first essential remains that throughout the free world there must be some rethinking about the blind, unreasoning condemnation of all things colonial and of the white man in Africa. Admittedly mistakes were made by the earlier colonisers, mistakes which the Rhodesias are today trying hard not only to put right but to atone for. This they cannot do by a sudden reckless abdication of their responsibilities, a fact which is more widely realised among responsible Africans than it appears to be in Europe or America.

While the Rhodesias can still, if allowed, set an example to the rest of Africa by building a healthy society capable of resisting the Russian and Chinese inroads, the Republic of South Africa can do less, if anything. The goodwill which exists in the Rhodesias is not present on a sufficiently large scale in South Africa, and the lack of goodwill has made that particular part of southern Africa a most vulnerable Soviet target.

Debasing the seriousness of the Communist drive in Africa by equalling, whether deliberately or through ignorance, every expression of liberal opinion with Communism, South African white nationalism has made itself a most valuable ally of Russia.

The rising dissatisfactions and frustrations of the vast non-white majority of the population, deprived of political, social and economic rights and increasingly subjected to restrictions and disabilities, have become the principal source of potential Communist strength in that country. The small nucleus of convinced Communists – both white and non-white – has already capitalised on the situation and has increased its influence in the leadership of such African trade unions as exist, and in all the most important non-white political organisations (African, Coloured and Indian).

Leaving South Africa aside, another Communist asset in Africa is the misery and corruption which have overtaken several of the more immature or irresponsibly-led newly independent countries. This, fortunately, is not a feature of the few parts still partly under European control. Just how quickly misery and corruption and injustice can come to a country was shown in the Congo, and may yet be shown in

Kenya – and also in Northern Rhodesia if the pressure against the white population continues.

Russia's Colonies

One consideration which makes the vigorous anti-colonialist campaign throughout the world suspected of being in fact a most successful Soviet manoeuvre is that one hears so little about the big colonies which lie outside Africa. If the United States and others are genuinely so concerned about colonialism, why is the decolonisation of Russia's colonies in Asia never demanded?

So far only one lone voice has spoken up for the people in these colonies. It is that of Leopold Senghor. Addressing a conference of the leaders of former French colonies in Africa, he drew attention to the vast part of Asia still under colonial rule – 'the colonies of the Tsars but which now form part of the U.S.S.R.' He added: 'The Soviet countries of Asia have been granted autonomy and have benefited from remarkable development but have not yet been granted independence.'

Not only do the critics of the continued presence of white men in parts of Africa say nothing about Russian colonialism, but they do nothing to counter Soviet propaganda to Africa which seeks to persuade the Africans that they can derive as much benefit from close association with Moscow as these Asian 'national republics' have derived. Nothing is said of the vicious suppression of political nationalism in the republics and the cruel persecution of any leader who is not unquestioningly subservient to Moscow.

What is known about it, which is enough, is conveniently ignored. The Russian Empire in very recent years has had its Kenyattas, Nkrumahs, Lumumbas and Kaundas. They have disappeared or have been executed, even under Khrushchev's liberal regime. One need only think of the pitiful attempts of

Kazakhstan, Uzbekistan, Bokhara, Turkestan and Khorezm to win some kind of national recognition, to develop some kind of balanced economy of their own, to preserve their own cultural heritage and language, and then remember the fate that has befallen their leaders and more articulate inhabitants.

Few Africans know the truth about these regions of the Soviet Union, and the so-called anti-colonialists in Britain and the United States do nothing to enlighten them.

British or French colonialism has nothing to compare with this history; these are examples of Russian colonialism as practised in the present day, by a regime whose leader can blandly tell Africans that colonialism is 'the most disgraceful form of man's oppression.' And this at a time when nationalism is forbidden in Soviet Central Asia, when the people concerned are not allowed unrestricted use of their own languages, and when their territories are being taken over by Russian settlers as part of Moscow's vast agricultural scheme, while large numbers of the local populations are deported.

Western colonialism was never as vicious as this, but not one word is heard about it at the United Nations or from Mr Mennon Williams in Washington. The Labour Party in Britain never speaks about it, nor does Mr Nehru, that other champion of oppressed peoples. If any of these people are concerned about the rapid advance Russia is making in Africa, here at least is the material with which a counter-attack can be started. Why are they so silent about it?

One single group of statistics should convince a few sceptics of the extent of Russian colonisation. Between 1933 and 1959 the Kazakh population of Kazakhstan fell from 57.1 per cent to *29.6 per cent*. During the same period the *Russian* population of Kazakhstan rose from 19.7 per cent to *43.1 per cent*. This is not even colonialism any more. It is part genocide and part imperialism on the pattern of Attila, applied with the velvet glove of a Ghengis Khan.

The Slave Trade

It is also high time that the ardent anti-colonialists in Britain and the United States stopped echoing Moscow in raking up the sad story of slavery. Slavery was not the invention of the early colonisers. It has been a phenomenon of all history and flourished in Africa long before the European colonisers arrived.

It was, indeed, for the specific purpose of fighting slavery that Britain moved into West and East Africa and thus rescued Ghana, Nigeria, Kenya, Zanzibar, Northern Rhodesia and the Sudan from the ravages of the slave trade. To do this the colonisers had to fight not only the Arab slave traders, but the African slave raiders. France did much the same. It is forgotten today that it was the British Government of the time which made the world conscious of the evils of slavery.

Now that the Europeans have gone from most of Africa, there is evidence in a number of places of a gradual resumption of slavery. Many Africans are aware of these facts and therefore do not share the current popular revulsion for colonialism. Instead of continuing the tirade against the evils of colonialism, let the United Nations investigate the recurrence of slavery.

The Quarrel in Guinea

At the time of writing the West is gleefully speculating about the seriousness of the alleged quarrel between Guinea and Russia and pointing out that the Soviet leaders have quite a few lessons still to learn in Africa. No doubt Russia *has* many lessons to learn: so has the West. But to hold up the case of Guinea as an example is puerile.

Daniel Solod, the former Soviet Ambassador in Guinea, had a personal quarrel with Sekou Touré because he meddled too much in the internal affairs of the country. He was asked to leave. His mistakes were to overlook the sensitiveness of

African nationalism, and his lack of patience. Degtyar, who has replaced him, is hardly less formidable.

Sekou Touré is today perhaps a disillusioned man. But Guinea's position as a Russian and Chinese forward base in Africa has not changed in the slightest. British colonial officials, and lately American officials, have had more serious quarrels with African leaders.

The only real effect of the Conakry quarrel will be that the Soviet leaders will have learnt a lesson and will not make the same mistake again – and as a result they will make fewer difficulties for themselves in future.

Time is Short

There remains only the hope that the time will come before it is too late when the new forces of idealism in the West will have matured enough to realise that the struggle for Africa *is* in progress and that some of the people in Africa, both black and white, are at least potential allies of the West while others have sold out to the Communist forces, are about to sell out or have genuinely embraced Russia or China.

In the first group, the whites and the blacks are not fighting each other everywhere and do not necessarily regard each other as enemies. Admittedly that does not always apply, but it should not be beyond the capacity of the leaders in Washington and London (and at the United Nations, should there be sufficient interest in the subject) to discover who is for them and who against.

Once they have done that, perhaps they will consider dropping many preconceived ideas about Africa. Then perhaps they will begin to discriminate between their friends and their enemies and accept it as a regrettable fact that it is now too late to win over Africa in its entirety.

When that is realised, there is still much that can be salvaged or saved. But time is running out – far too much has run out already, and every inch of ground lost will be almost impossible to regain.

There is far too much irresponsible opportunism in the West. When you are on the defensive there is no room for opportunism. At this stage it is something which only Moscow and Peking can afford to indulge in. The West, in fact, may soon have its back to the wall in Africa.

POSTSCRIPT

By means of extraordinary self-deception many political leaders at the United Nations, in Washington and in London still talk as if it is possible to keep the cold war out of Africa; as if the policy of leaving Africa on the side lines is actually succeeding.

The more enlightened and more responsible African leaders sincerely wish to be left out of the general world struggle, but unfortunately they do not set the pace.

The Belgrade neutralist summit conference in September 1961, which was in effect an attempt to create a third world bloc which would be fully involved in the cold war, was well attended by African leaders, and nobody seemed to find it incongruous that of all people, Adoula from the Congo should lecture the world on the state in which it finds itself.

Even many realists who have for some time been aware of the developing nightmare which Africa represents as a cold war battleground have been taken by surprise. The speed and extent of the Communist offensive have been greater than even they expected. Few were able to foresee that a stage would be reached so soon in which the *World Marxist Review* could claim, with apparent satisfaction, that 'today Africa is a raging conflagration in which the last hopes of the colonialists are going up in smoke.'

The cold war is waged in Africa with perhaps a greater intensity than anywhere else, and is supported by Russia and China with every device at their disposal. One undoubted Communist objective is to reduce European influence to zero, and lately this appears to have become a United Nations objective as well. Unfortunately it also seems to have become an American aim.

For Communism this objective is entirely logical. In the case of a world war, it would be disastrous for the West if Africa did not hold out; with European influence removed, the prospects of that continent holding out in the conditions of a global war, are nil.

But even the cold war Communist conquest of Africa cannot be completed while a definite European influence remains. It is possible that it is only direct and indirect European influence which stands between what order there now is in some countries in Africa and chaos on the Congo pattern. If the United Nations had not pursued its policy to expel the European factor from the Congo with such vigour, even that country might have been spared some at least of the tragedy that has befallen her.

The true nature of much of the African struggle today should not be obscured by the great volume of propaganda. It is not primarily a struggle between African and European. It is to a far greater extent a struggle between African and African, and it is at its most intense where European influence has been expelled altogether.

In Nigeria, Senegal, (French) Congo, Ivory Coast and a number of other places where the leaders continue voluntarily to seek European co-operation, conditions are far healthier than in those territories where hatred of the former colonial Powers has become almost pathological. In this last connection the Congo, Ghana, Guinea, Somalia and others immediately come to mind.

It would be of interest to know how many Americans in a position to give leadership do not to some extent agree with Plyshevsky's criticism of what he believes European policy to be. 'The imperialists are compelled,' he has written, 'to retreat and manoeuvre in order to combat the steadily growing national-liberation movement of the colonial peoples. Aware that they cannot maintain the colonial system in its old form, the imperialists are forced to grant independence as a safety valve, a strategic move designed to prevent, or at least put off, complete loss of colonial possessions.

'But in granting political independence to their colonies, the imperialists . . . endeavour to emasculate and undermine the national sovereignty of the new countries, to misrepresent the principle of self-determination of nations, to impose new forms of colonial domination under the spurious slogan of 'independence,' install their puppets in these countries and corrupt a section of the *bourgeoisie*. They resort to the poisoned weapon of national strife to undermine the young States that are not yet strong enough.

'At the same time, they do not hesitate to embark on colonial wars whenever the monopolies are determined to retain their hold on a colony and all other methods of doing so are of no avail.'

If the United States did not share at least some of Plyshevsky's views, then her record concerning the Congo, especially Katanga, would probably have been different. She would then at least have registered protest when it appeared as if the United Nations had taken Plyshevsky's words as its guiding light.

The same applies to at least a part of British public opinion.

In deciding its Katanga policy, the United Nations seemingly had in mind the following advice from the *World Marxist Review*: 'The support which we should extend to the people of Africa . . . does not mean that we keep silent about the policy pursued by some of the African leaders, a policy which, in our view, runs counter to the interests of the people of Africa . . . We are convinced that the arbitrary and anti-democratic policy of some of the African governments which have launched an anti-Communist crusade are at variance with the genuine national interests of these countries and the struggle of the people generally.'

Katanga occupied a very special place. It was much more developed than the rest of the Congo, with which it was grouped almost accidentally, and it was unique in being exceptionally prosperous. Economically and to some extent geographically, and certainly in the political thinking of Moise Tshombe, it belonged to southern Africa rather than to the emerging central Africa. For that reason it had to be singled out for special treatment – by Moscow, by the United Nations and seemingly, by Washington. It had either to be bottled up or destroyed.

The United Nations did not only bring chaos to Katanga. It also placed on the borders of the Central African Federation, within a stone's throw of the richest part of Northern Rhodesia, forces which are under the indirect control of Moscow or Moscow's allies, open or clandestine.

All that now supports the continuance of law, order and prosperity in Northern Rhodesia is the fact that she still has a strong Government determined to keep her as a Western bastion. But, like Katanga before her, she seems destined for destruction or isolation. The termites are already at work. So also are many Africans within the territory who are ready to bring chaos to one of the few remaining really orderly countries in Africa.

A question which nags constantly is whether the free world really is collectively concerned about the fate of Africa. If it is, then the make-belief approach of both London and Washington – that the cold war is being kept out of Africa, that Africa can also be kept out of a shooting war if it should break out, that the Communist bloc's influence can be kept out of most of Africa, that the only thing wrong with Africa is that there are still a number of Europeans in it, and so on – becomes inexplicable. America's ignorance of Africa may be a partial explanation. A similar plea of ignorance will not do as an excuse for Britain.

It is sometimes suggested that some men in policy-making positions in the West are secretly pro-Communist. I do not accept this, but there seems little doubt that key persons sometimes fall victim to the steady Communist propaganda inundation. This is possible because so few of the facts are easily available. Ignorance of what is happening behind the scenes in Africa, and consequent confused thinking, is possibly the most serious charge that can be made against London and Washington.

But even if they mean well the outcome is just as disastrous if, almost continuously, wrong policy decisions are made. Often, too, there is justification for suspecting that policy decisions are dictated by fear and made by men who are weak.

INDEX